Create a World Class Soccer Defense

A 100 Soccer Drills, Tactics and Techniques to Shutout the Competition

Chest Dugger

Table Of Contents

ABOUT THE AUTHOR

Chest Dugger is a pen name for our soccer coaching brand, Abiprod. We provide high quality soccer coaching tips, drills, fitness and mentality tips to ensure your success.

We have been fans of the beautiful game for decades. Like every soccer fan around the globe, we watch and play the beautiful game as much as we can. Whether we're fans of Manchester United, Real Madrid, Arsenal or LA Galaxy; we share a common love for the beautiful game. Through our experiences, we've noticed that there's very little information for the common soccer fan who wants to escalate his game to the next level. Or get their kids started on the way. Too much of the information on the web and outside is too basic.

Being passionate about the game, we want to get the message across to as many people as possible. Through our soccer coaching blog, books and products; we aim to bring high quality soccer coaching to the world. Anyone who's passionate about the beautiful game can use our tactics and strategies.

Here's a link to our author page for other books:

DISCLAIMER

Introduction

The English Premier League is the wealthiest soccer league in the world. As this book started to take shape the 2019 summer transfer window had just ended. The three biggest purchases made by teams in this league, funded by huge commercial enterprises, unbelievable wealthy owners and extravagant amounts of TV money were:

Third: Manchester City filled the gap in their defensive midfield which will grow ever bigger as their talismanic Brazilian, Fernandhino, ages. Rodri, from Atletico Madrid is the man they hope will protect a back line they need to be secure if they are to satisfy their goal to conquer Europe. He cost the super-rich, Saudi financed club around $76 million.

Second: Nicholas Pepe from Lorient to Arsenal. The North London outfit paid the equivalent of $87 million for the exciting young winger. Pepe has an outstanding scoring record for a wide player, outperformed in the net finding stakes only by Kirian Mbappe in the French Ligue 1 in the 2018-19 season.

First: Here comes the shock. Manchester United were prepared to pay Leicester City the equivalent of just a fraction under $100 million for Harry Maguire. Now big Harry is a fine player. An England international, he is strong in the air and accomplished on the ground. But, as those familiar with European soccer will know, Maguire is not some pacy winger, a goal getting center forward or even a sublime creative midfielder. He is a center back. The most expensive player purchased in the wealthiest league in the world plays in defense.

So, two out of the three biggest signings in this transfer window are defensively minded. The world is changing.

Everything Needs Protection

And, it would seem, that includes the US. In fact, the Government of the United States seems to feel more strongly about defense than any other nation in the world. At least in terms of money it is prepared to push in the way of preventing other countries and terrorist organizations put an unwanted ball in its very large net, so to speak.

The US defense budget for 2019 is a stagger $717 billion, according to army-technology.com. That is more than four times the size of the next largest budget. (Which is, incidentally, that of China, who are the only other nation to commit more than $100 million towards protecting their nation, coughing up $177 billion. Third,

7

somewhat surprisingly, are India, whose $60 billion commitment is one twelfth of the size of the liability met by inhabitants of the likes of Ohio and Oregon.)

Still, this is meant to be a book about soccer, and as fascinating as the relative worth different nations place on protecting themselves might be, it is relevant to the soccer pitch only in an analogical sense.

Our point is that defense is an essential part of life. It is not the most glamourous. It tends to be an aspect of existence upon which little time is spent. But without it, we are in trouble. Whether it be to hackers determined to upload our bank details from our phones, terrorists seeking to cause mayhem in an attempt to tell their one-sided story or ensuring a single goal is enough to win a match, defense is vital.

Clearly, ensuring our houses are safe against burglars is immeasurably more important than preventing a corner from ending up in the back of the net. Even (we'd hope) to the most ardent of fans.

But despite that, comparisons can be drawn. Just as a huge air force is insufficient as the main line of national defense in an era when attacks are likely to seditious rather than overt – a bomb in a subway or a cyber-attack on a hospital; just as we need more than a hi-tech bolt to block out the determined burglar, so soccer defense is developing in the face of the threat of more subtle and intelligent offensive play.

Responding to the Development of Offense

Rarely these days do teams base their offense around a giant striker looking to nod down long balls to a teammate. Offense is based around more complex routines. For example, the vital role of transition, where speed and movement are used to exploit the space created by defensive players having moved forward and out of position. Or the intricacies of number 10s who can thread a pass through a spyhole in a door for their speedy fellow strikers to move onto.

And so, soccer defense is evolving to deal with this. The aforementioned Harry Maguire is a big man. He is good in the air and his bulk makes him a menace to opposing offenses. In that sense, he is like the battleship, or the solid front door – defense of old. But he is also fast; he can bring the ball under control and dribble out of defense, turning pressure on his goal into an attack on another; he is a danger at corners and set pieces – just like defenders of yore – but he can also play a perfectly weighted thirty meter pass directly into the run of a team mate.

The likes of Harry Maguire are the result of the evolution of defense in soccer. They are players capable of being old fashioned stoppers, yet also ones who can show a turn of pace, and crucially also compliment their team's offense. But, as Manchester United realized this summer, they come at a price.

Shhh – Don't Shout About It, But Defenses Win Matches, Leagues and Cups

Now for some facts to digest. In the most recent completed season, 2018-19, here are the defensive records of the winners and runners up of various leagues:

Spain, La Liga: Winners Barcelona (36 goals conceded – third lowest), second Atletico Madrid (29 conceded, fewest in the league).

Germany, the Bundesliga: Winners Bayern Munich (no surprises there, but they conceded just 32 goals, the second lowest in the league). Second placed Borussia Dortmund's goal was breached the fourth fewest of times, 34. The best defensive record came from third placed RB Leipzig, with a miserly 29 conceded, including just nine in seventeen matches at home.

Italy, Serie A. Juventus secured the title well before the end of the season and failed to win any of their final five games. Nevertheless, they won the league by eleven points, conceding just thirty times on the way. That was the lowest in the league. Second placed Napoli were third placed in the defensive stakes, being breached on only thirty-six occasions.

In the runaway Premier league, champions Manchester City had the second meanest defense, with just twenty-three conceded in thirty-eight matches. Second placed Liverpool topped the defense league, conceding one less than their rivals. Third placed Chelsea were not only twenty-five points further back but were also breached by seventeen more goals.

It is not just in the major leagues where this key defensive fact applies. In the Greek Super league champions Paok conceded just fourteen goals in winning the title. That is less than one in every two games. The Norwegian Tippeligaen was still being played at the time of writing, but in 2018 champions Rosenburg also topped, or bottomed as might be a better description, the goals conceded chart with just twenty-four in thirty matches.

Although there is a correlation between scoring the most goals and winning leagues, it does not seem to be quite as strong as having a watertight defense. For example, Juventus were third in the scoring stakes in Italy, some way behind the top two. (They netted seventy times, the top two were seventy-seven – Atalanta – and seventy-four for Napoli.) In Belgium, champions KRC Genk were only joint seventh in home goals scored (they were second with home goals conceded, although their away scoring record was much stronger.)

In Romania, CFR Cluj topped the La Liga, but were merely fifth with home goals scored and third overall. However, they conceded far less than any of their opponents.

So, we might conclude that while scoring goals thrills the crowd and helps a team to win, to be a champion it is even more important that the defense is as strong as it can possibly be.

We hope that we have made our case. Defense is key to a team's success. But there is another important reason for this coaching book on a team's defensive unit. We can coach attacking play; set moves, individual skills and so forth can all help a team to create and score chances. However, goals often result from a touch of magic. The thirty-yard screaming shot; the piece of dribbling brilliance, the through pass hit with precision and vision. These are hard attributes to coach. Or they can result from an error by the opposition. A mishit clearance, a goal keeping mistake, a positional defect or communication lapse.

The coach can make a bigger impact with defense than he or she can with offensive players. Movement that becomes second nature, knowledge, technique, experience and positional awareness – allied to teamwork and communication – these are the elements that come together to produce a defense hard to breach. They are all factors which the coach can improve with their team through drills, team and individual coaching.

It is true, if not often said, that attackers thrill the crowd while defenders win matches, at whatever level we play the game, from professional to Under ten teams playing on a Sunday morning. And it is there, with the match winning defense, that a coach earns his salt.

The Basic Principles of Defending

It might be said that there are four elements to any game of soccer:

- The time our team are in possession – offense
- The time we are out of possession – defense
- The time possession changes – transition
- The time neither side is in possession because the ball is out of play.

We can interpret the tactics of defense in many ways; each coach has his or her own favoured approach, and since no one method has emerged to dominate it is fair to conclude that there is no absolute when it comes to doing things right or wrong.

In our approach, we will break defense down into two extremely broad constituent parts: team defending and individual defending. Later chapters will look at aspects of these in greater detail, but in this chapter, we will be looking at the fundamental principles of each.

By definition, therefore, the tips, skills and drills will be basic. However, that does not limit them to use with youth teams and beginners to the game. Even at the highest international level, defenders make fundamental mistakes which cost their team goals, and games.

A session working on basic techniques will help to reinforce the fundamentals of this element of the game with every defender and should be incorporated into every coach's programme.

(Note: some of the following 100 drills, tactics and techniques include diagrams.)

In these:

White Circle = Defense

Black Circle = Offense

Black Circle with a G inside = Goalkeeper

Black Circle with an N inside = Neutral player

Circles with other letters or numbers – Players with clarifications

Grey Circle = Extra team if needed

Small Grey Circle = Ball

Black Line = Movement of the ball

White Line = Movement of the player

Grey Line = Player dribbling ball

One (Tactic): When to practise basic principles of defense?
Clearly, the coach will look at the level and experience of his team
before deciding on the answer to this question. We recommend that for
youth teams, up to Under 12s, every training session should have one
'basic principle' drill. For more experienced youth teams, and adult
teams, a recap on basics should be fitted into the coach's programme at
least once a month, to keep the concepts fresh in the players' minds.

On top of this, at any level, coaches should be prepared to adapt
their plan to offer additional drills and focus sessions when the evidence
from matches highlights the need.

For example, if during a game our side gives away too many free kicks, it may be necessary to add in drills on tackling to the next coaching session. This ability to be fluid with planning, while retaining a basic structure to a session is a key attribute of every good coach.

Principles of Team Defending

We might break down the highly complex nature of team defending to the following key aims:

- Deny the opposing team space;
- Force the opposition to play the ball under pressure;
- As a team, pressure the ball, support the first defender, mark a space or a man.

Two (Drill): Simple drill to deny the opposing team space:

This drill looks complex but is simple. There are three teams of four, plus two neutral players who always join the side of the team in possession. There are two goalkeepers who are also part of the team in possession.

The aim of the offensive teams (here marked in black and grey) is to get the ball passed from one goalkeeper to the other. The ball must be played at least once in each grid, including the narrow space in the middle.

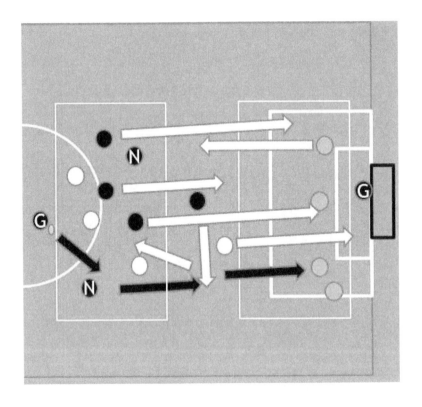

The offensive teams line up as above. As the ball is played into the central area, one player from the other end (grey above) moves into the central area. When the black player has played the ball into the grey zone, he must retreat into his own zone.

The white defender in the central area attempts to slow downplay until his teammates can sprint from the zone with the black team's attackers, to the one with the grey defenders. They should aim to get behind the ball and stay narrow.

The nearest defender (which will usually be the one who has been in the central area) should press the ball to slow down the attack. One white defender moves to replace this player in the central zone.

The coach encourages his defense to sprint into position, to communicate as to who will press, and who will mark. The tackle is not made unless either a) the attacker loses control or b) the defense is in place.

The offense can play the ball from end to end as often as they like, as long as the ball is played through the central zone. However, they only succeed when both goalkeepers touch the ball. If possession is lost the defenders swap with the attackers who last touched the ball.

Three (Drill): Force the opposition to play the ball under pressure:

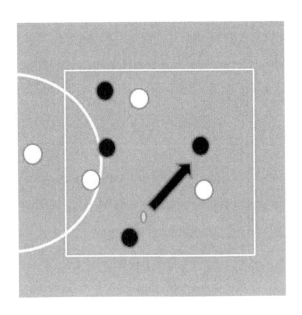

Here, there are 4 v 4 players, the defense has one player outside the grid. The aim is for the attackers to keep possession with their extra player within the grid. The defense must win possession. If they get the ball out of the grid, the attack starts once more. After five restarts, the teams swap. If the defense win the ball and play it to their teammate outside the grid, possession changes immediately.

The coach encourages communication and constant movement from the defense. The nearest player closes the ball to force a pass; the other two defense players mark the nearest opponent to make the pass as hard as possible. The outside defender moves to support should possession change hands.

Four (Tactics and Drills): Knowing our jobs when defending as a team:

One of the issues with running drills is that, as close to real life as we can make them, they are still somewhat artificial. Teaching our defense its job (and here, we mean defense in the widest possible terms) does require match practice.

We can discuss, stress and outline the way in which we want our defense to operate. The fundamentals we will use will include:

1) Nearest player presses;
2) Second player supports;
3) Other players mark a space or another player;
4) Communication helps to ensure that runs are picked up;
5) We concentrate on maintaining shape position;
6) We avoid defending too deep.

However, there can be a substantial difference between theory and practice. The best way to ensure that our defense operates as we wish it to make it a focus of full team and large side practices. Stop sessions to point out strengths and weaknesses. Encourage leadership by getting the team involved in communicating instructions.

How Many Players On A Team Are Defenders?

The answer, without wishing to sound too trite, is eleven. (Which is, of course, the same answer as to the question 'How many players on a team are offensive?')

One of the most popular current trends in defending, at professional level at least, is the high press. Although a defensive measure, in as much as it is a tactic used when out of possession, it has at its heart an attacking philosophy. We can see through a tactical look at the differences between the high press and more traditional, deep defending why in both cases all eleven players on the team become a part of the defense when the team is out of possession.

Five (Tactic): Traditional Defending; getting behind the ball.

Here, when out of possession the team drops back to a given line, pre-determined by the coach before the game. The aim is slow down the build-up of the opposition, allowing the majority, or even all, of the team to get behind the ball (i.e. – between the ball and the goal) to narrow space in the danger zone.

The opposition are permitted space on the ball when far from goal and will often keep possession by playing lateral passes. However, when trying to create a goal scoring chance, the defense is packed and space is minimal. This means breaking through such a defense is extremely difficult.

The strengths of this system lie solely in stopping the opposition from scoring. Lack of space, cover should errors be made and the relative simplicity of simply dropping back behind the ball make it a popular method of defense. The disadvantage is that when play eventually breaks down and the defense regain possession, they usually do so from a deep position, with their players far from their opponent's goal. Although teams try to counter this by leaving one player 'up', this striker can become very isolated.

Six (Tactic): The high press

By contrast, the high press is a riskier and more challenging defensive approach. However, because it is becoming the system of choice for an increasing number of teams, we have included it in the 'basic principles' chapter.

Here, the defensive line is the ball. There is no dropping off to give the opponents space. The strikers pressure the ball intensively, making the defender on the ball either play the ball hastily, and therefore risk a bad pass, or play it long and give away possession.

The advantage of this system is that if transition occurs, the side winning possession are already in an advanced position, and therefore can increase their chances of making a goal scoring opportunity before the defense can re-organise.

Since the press is high up the pitch, it is defenders whose passing is put under pressure, and they are less likely to be able to cope with this than a talented passing midfielder, who may be the one to make the key pass in the defensive system outlined in Tactic Five.

However, there are downsides with the approach. Firstly, if the high press fails, then the side in possession will have greater space to play the ball since three or four 'defenders' are already far up the pitch. Therefore, everybody must know their job and do it; there is a much smaller margin for error in defending this way.

Secondly, the players pressing (who are nearly always strikers, since it is their part of the pitch where the press takes place) must be extremely fit. They will need to run hard to close down players and chase the ball. If, for example, four players are involved in the press, and one falls off the pace, the defenders in possession suddenly have their own time and space and can exploit their opponent's own defensive third.

We will look in more detail at drills to develop an effective high press in the 'Team Shape' chapter later in the book.

Principles of Individual Defending

We might break down the principles of individual defending into three broad categories:

- The hold up: Here, defenders slow down the opponent in possession to allow team mates to recover their own positions. Players will try to steer opponents into the area of least threat; this might be away from goal, or into an area where the defense is well set and crowded.
- Closing the door: Here the defense denies their opponents space. This can be both directly linked to the ball, and also to space into which the ball might be played. Defenders will follow such tactics as direct their opponent onto their

weaker foot, block the shot or pass and work to position themselves to force a pass either away from goal or into a well defended area.

- Stealing the ball: Or, the tackle.

Seven (Drill): Basic drill for holding up an opponent:

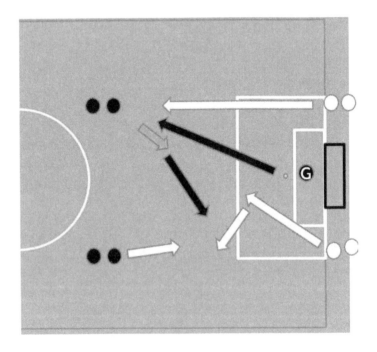

This is a great drill for promoting teamwork and communication. The goalkeeper kicks the ball to one of the two strikers, about 35-45 yards from goal. The nearest defender sprints to close down the space for this striker; the other defender moves under more control to a covering position. He or she can then support the first defender, while also cover a pass.

When the pass is made to the other attacker (if that is how the drill develops), the cover defender becomes the main defender, sprinting to cover the pass. The first defender now becomes the cover.

Coaches can set a time limit within which the strikers must get away a shot. Players rotate after each attempt.

Eight (Drill): Blocking Shots and Passes

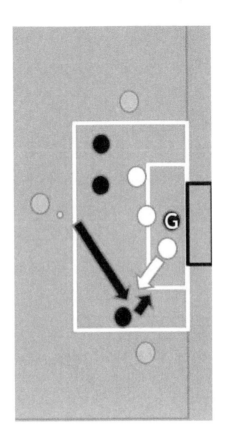

Three teams of two, three or four players are required, plus a goalkeeper and plenty of balls. One team (grey) feeds the ball into the penalty area. The blacks must get in a shot, while the whites attempt to block shots and passes. Switch the teams regularly and, with younger players, keep an eye on safety.

The key techniques for the defense are:

1) An attitude and determination to win the ball. What we might call 'heart'. This is instilled through lots of positive feedback from the coach and teammates.

2) Press the ball quickly;

3) With the newly clarified laws on handball, ensure that arms are in a natural position, and are not actively making the body area larger than it would normally be. There is no need today to approach with arms behind the defender's back. In any case, that is a technique which puts the player at risk of injury.

4) Ensure that the defender runs at the correct angle to the ball. Their body should be in line with the ball and its intended target.

Nine (Drill): Forcing players onto their weaker foot

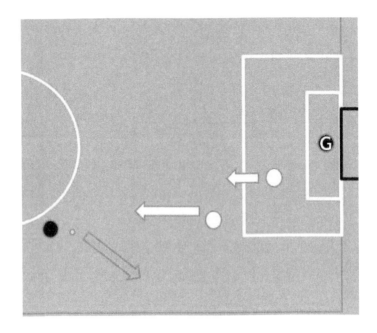

This is a very easy drill to operate and deliver, but gets players thinking about limiting risk by forcing players onto their weaker foot.

To begin with, the drill can be 1 v 1 in a grid. This was, there can be high involvement from the squad, with several duels taking place at once. The attacker dribbles the ball, the defender approaches as per normal, but instead of getting in line, the defender positions themselves so that they offer greater space to the player's weaker side. They should be shoulder on to the player but located so they cannot easily be turned.

The drill can develop, as above, with extra players. For example, the covering defender also offers greatest space to the weaker side.

Ten (Drill): Covering space:

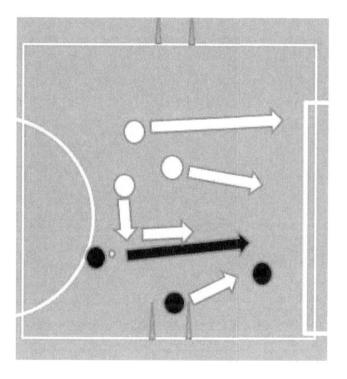

This drill involves a large grid with two small goals at each end. Two small sided teams, three or four per side, compete, the offense's aim is to dribble the ball through the goals while the drill helps the defense to develop their skills in covering.

The basic principle of the nearest man closing the ball applies while his teammates cover the space behind them. Their intention is to keep the offense playing in front of them. The coach stops the game frequently to point out good and bad tactical movement from the defense, and to use questioning (WHY did you move there? HOW will you protect the space behind you?) to develop leadership skills in the players.

Eleven (Drill): Block tackling

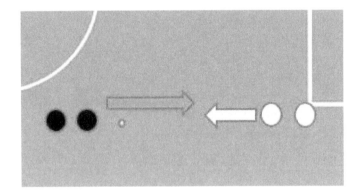

Soccer is a simple game. Sometimes the best drills are also the simplest. Here we simply practise the block tackle with a series of 1 v 1 dribbles and tackles. Another reason to avoid complex drills with tackling exercises is the risk of injury. When less is going on, the risk of error leading to injury is reduced.

The key elements of the technique of block tackling are:

1) The defender approaches steadily and under control;
2) Weight is forward and the player is on their toes and with their knees slightly bent;
3) Arms are out for balance;
4) The 'block' prevents the pass or the attempt to move past the defender; it often occurs when the attacking player slightly loses control of the ball, so it moves too far in front of them;
5) The tackle is made with the head over the tackling foot to maximise weight in the tackle;
6) The leg should NOT be fully extended for this tackle, as the impact is heavy and there is a risk of injury to ankle and knee.

Twelve (Drill): Sliding Tackles

If all tackling is risky when it comes to injury, the slide tackle is more so. Therefore, in drills we wish to avoid contact.

For that reason, we practise on a moving ball only.

The focus of the drill is technique and we move from the poke tackle, where the ball is poked away from the attacker, to the full sliding tackle:

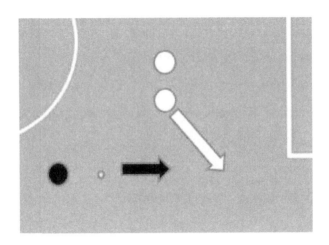

1) For the poke, approach from the side or front. Tackling from behind is illegal even if the ball is won;

2) Lean in with the shoulder;

3) Head forward, extend the leading foot to poke the ball away;

4) Ensure the leg is bent at the knee;

5) When this technique is strong, move on to the full sliding tackle;

6) Approach from the side – a sliding tackle from the front or rear is dangerous play;

7) Extend the leading leg so that it remains bent, with the studs facing downwards;

8) Fall to the ground and extend further as contact is made;

9) Ensure the head is still and watching the ball.

The sliding tackle, as spectacular as it looks, is the tackle of last resort. Mis timed it can result in injury, a yellow or red card and the tackler is out of the game.

Here are the key points from the chapter:

- Every player on the team should view themselves as a part of the defense;
- Defense is what happens when we are out of possession;
- There are two key elements to defense – team defense and individual defense;
- Core, basic skills and tactics should be drilled, even with experienced player.

In the next chapter we will turn our attention to one of the great debates between defense coaches – the relative benefits of a zonal approach against a man marking system.

The Difference Between Man to Man and Zonal Defending

It's probably in the words. There's something tough, hard bitten in the idea of man to man marking. Conflict in the trenches, survival of the strongest. We picture hard faced Italians kicking their talented but lightweight opponents off the park. Chisel jawed Chileans, uncompromising in the tackle and up to all the tricks of the trade behind the watchful eye of the officials.

We are also far too sophisticated for such hard line defense. We are the liberal metropolitan elite – we believe in higher values. Yet we hold a sneaking admiration for the tough guy man to man marker. It is a style for the men's game. It's not called women to women marking, for goodness sake. As for the youth side of the sport – get real. Child to child marking seems like a recipe for the involvement of a team of social workers.

Still, if our nattily coiffured number ten is hacked out of the game by a six-foot two lump of muscle with the soccer skills of a donkey but the heart of a lion, we complain at the time, but it is half hearted. In truth, we hold more than a slight wish that the game was still so simple.

Man to man marking is the system from history, the throwback to happier, less complicated times. It is the closest (other than the World Cup) soccer gets to xenophobia.

In contrast, zonal marking is for woolly hearted wussies. The sort who use Alice bands in their hair and wear cycle shorts beneath their kit. It is sanitised soccer for the snowflake generation. Teams who use it lack heart and leadership and are guaranteed to fold under the slightest pressure. It is the defense system of the artists – pretty on the surface but meaningless underneath.

Or at least, the above is the story we hear in the media. Ex-pros love to boast of the game in their day, where the match had been a non-event if both your legs were still attached by the end of the game. 'We're forgetting it's a contact sport,' they mutter, deepening their voice and sticking out their (slightly paunchy) torsos. During their time a victory had nothing to do with the score, but involved escaping the swinging limbs of Big Billy MacSmackYerFace, back from an eight-match ban for using an upturned linesman as a corner flag.

'Zonal marking never works…' they moan as replays of a headed goal are shown to the audience.

Naturally, the story told so far holds little relation to the truth. Man marking is what it says on the tin, a defense arrangement where an individual player is charged with stopping an opponent from doing their job. It can work at various levels of intensity. Many teams will man mark from set pieces, pairing for example, their best header of a ball against their opponent's to reduce the danger from a corner, free kick or throw in.

At other times a side may switch to man marking when play enters a certain part of the pitch. At the very highest levels, where all players have a high degree of skill, man marking is rarely used in the modern game beyond set pieces, but lower down the pyramid teams may set out with the intention of stopping a particular player whom they identify as a special threat. It may be that one player sits on the shoulder of this threat throughout the game (a thankless task, almost certain to end with a booking and little pleasure) or different players assume responsibility as the threat enters their area of the pitch.

Most fans will probably agree that the greatest player to ever step on to a soccer field was the Brazilian master, Pele. As part of the multi-talented Brazil of 1970 he was man of the tournament as they strode towards victory. He should have dominated more of these competitions. He had participated as a young teenager in 1958, giving evidence of his talent. By 1962, Pele was the world's best player, even though he was just twenty-one years old. That made him a target, and he went unprotected by officials. Injuries mounted and he played very little. In 1966 a similar story ensued.

The sixties and seventies were the heyday of man marking. Perhaps it is no surprise that the system has such an unpleasant reputation. In fact, as we shall see, there are times when its use makes sense.

Zonal marking is more sophisticated and requires greater attention to detail. Again, it is used mostly in dead ball situations but can also underpin the team defensive shape when coaches require it to do so.

What we will seek to achieve in this chapter is to make a case for the strengths and weaknesses of both systems, with drills to practise them. We will conclude that the best defenses employ a combination of both set ups.

Man Marking

Thirteen (Tactic): Targeting an individual:

Coaches might decide that one player on the opposing team represents such a serious threat that they need special attention. In that case, a player may be allocated to man mark the opponent throughout the game. This marker needs the following attributes:

- To have the concentration and discipline to stay close to his opponent at all times;
- To stay goal side in the final third;
- Since the opponent will be most threatening during transition, to remain close enough on these occasions to prevent the player finding space;
- To be a player who stays on his or her feet; diving in is risky in any situation, but when man marking a player who dives in risks both a yellow card AND being left on the floor and out of the game. If the player being marked was not already ultra-talented, then there would be no need to man mark him.

Fourteen (Tactic): Man marking an individual based on zones

The skills are as above, but the coach must make it clear which person on his team has responsibility for the marking, and at what position on the pitch that responsibility comes into play. Often, and effectively, the 'nearest player' will be given the role. However, there is a risk that the target will use their ability to find spaces making it hard for him to be marked.

Mesut Ozil, the Arsenal and former German international, is one of the game's finest passers. It is interesting to watch the approaches opponents use to reduce his impact. Some simply pack the final third, restricting the space into which he can pass; others try to deny him access to the ball by cutting out through passes to him. Most will try to mark him in the final third, giving responsibility to the nearest player.

It is in these situations that Ozil is often most effective. He has the ability to drift between defensive lines, and so to mark him another player is pulled out of position, creating space for teammates.

Man Marking from Set Pieces

In the modern game, it is usually from these dead ball scenarios that man marking is employed. We have all witnessed the tussles in the penalty areas as players attempt to find space away from their markers, while the defense seeks to ensure that does not happen. Nearly always, from corners and close to the box free kicks, there is offending by one team or other. Frequently both.

It was interesting to note the use of VAR (the video assistant referee) in the 2018 World Cup in Russia. In the early stages a lot of attention was given to fouls in the box from dead ball situation, with many penalties ensuing. As the tournament developed, coaches realised that their defense would need to be more careful – simply hanging on to an opponent would be spotted by the VAR and punished. As a result, defense policy changed.

However, for most of us, the prospect of seeing VAR employed in the matches we play in or coach for is remote indeed. Therefore, man marking perhaps plays a bigger role than for highly monitored top level professional games.

Fifteen (Tactic): Man marking from dead balls

The following tactics should be considered by the coach:

- Match up strong headers of the ball against the strongest on the opponent's team;
- Retain, though, a tall player to cut out the near post corner, heading it away before it reaches the danger zone.
  - This means that corner takers will need to get more height on their crosses, which inevitably means

43

less whip and velocity (or the ball will fly out of play). In these situations, the keeper has more opportunity to intercept the ball.

- Bear in mind that opponents will be aiming for one of their players, and will employ their own men to try to disrupt the man marking from taking place;

- It is not always necessary to win the header, just being a disruptive presence will often lead to the attacker missing the ball, or target.

- Be aware of the near post danger. A whipped ball into this area becomes very hard to defend after a flick on. That flick on can just as easily come off the head of a marker as an attacker. Therefore, the player defending this area should be good in the air, and physically strong to stand up to the bustle that occurs there.

Sixteen (Drill): Man marking in open play:

This is a drill best worked on during a match practice or small sided game. While the focus of such a session will be on some other tactic or skill, allocate one or two players the specific role of man marking. Stop the game frequently to assess the positioning of the man marker.

Also, vary the man marking from whole pitch, to final third, defensive half and so forth.

However, the drill above does work well for specific man marking practice. Each team has a sweeper – the white sweeper may only patrol the area behind the edge of the box, and black sweeper is a get out player based in the centre circle. No other players are allowed in this space.

Blacks try to create a shot on goal; whites defend. White may intercept or block a pass but not tackle.

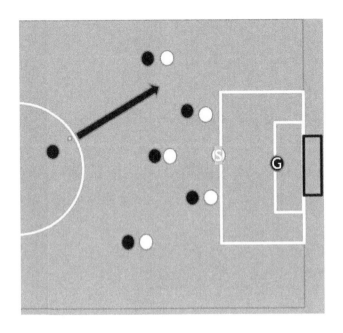

Seventeen (Drill): Man marking from corners and free kicks

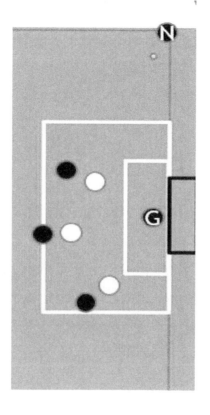

If the skill level or age of the team dictates, then the 'corner' can be simulated with throws into the box.

The defense should each be goal side of the man they are marking. They should be aware of the fake run, where the striker takes a step in one direction, before reversing into space. In a match situation, attempts will be made to stop a player being marked. Usually, this will be by blocking a marker in a crowded situation.

If illegally blocked, the defender should go to ground. This is not simulation, since they are the player being fouled, and that should be brought to the referee's attention. A low body position, with arms out for balance, makes blocking a man marking run more difficult.

Technique:

1) Watch the player more than the ball – every glance at the ball gives the striker a chance to move;
2) However, awareness of the ball must still be maintained;
3) Keep within arm's length of the man to be marked;
4) Keep a low body position, on toes with knees slightly bent so direction can be changed, and a quick start made;
5) Be sure to remain directly goal side unless we can certainly win the ball, then poke in front of our man.
6) Even if we cannot win the ball, we remain a presence by jumping or lunging to block the header or shot. The distraction will make it harder for our target to hit his target.

Zonal Marking

As the name suggests, zonal marking means that each player has an area which they must defend. Often, the attacker will win the ball with zonal defending, but the lack of space in which they win the ball will mean that they do not score or create a goal scoring chance.

Eighteen (Tactic): Zonal marking at corners:

From set plays, a line will be set. From corners, this will often be on the edge or just inside the six-yard box. A player will cover the area outside the near post, another covers the space level with the near post. Two or three players cover the central area and a final one looks after the far post and area beyond it. As can be seen, this type of marking is player intensive, which denies space in the box. A crowded penalty area is favourable to the defense.

Nineteen (Tactic): Zonal marking from free kicks.

This is usually employed when free kicks are wide. Since offside now comes into play, the defensive line will be set as far forward as possible. Often, the edge of the box is used. This allows the keeper time and space to collect a ball in behind the defensive line.

Coaches will use training sessions to practise zonal line ups from various positions, so players know where to position themselves in the game.

There are strengths and weaknesses with the system.

- Space is denied to opponents;
- There is less chance of a free header than with man marking, since the defense is not reliant on a single individual against another individual;
- The delivery of the pass is even more important (and difficult) because it must not only find its man, but also miss out the zonal line.
- On the other hand, the system can lead to very static defending. Attackers will be running onto the ball, and therefore able to get greater momentum coming into the contact with the ball. This means they can get a better jump, or more speed to win a 50-50 situation.

We have, with tongue in cheek, considered the war stories of ex pros with a grudge against a game that is leaving them behind (not all fit this category, but it is notable to view post-match analysis from this kind of player, and the ex-coach who is on the panel...), The fact is that neither system is perfect. Statistically, at the professional level, zonal marking is marginally, very marginally, more successful in stopping goals than man marking. However, at the amateur level, the chance to get away with more 'interference' probably swings the monitor just towards man marking. We have no statistics for this, but common sense suggests it is true.

On the other hand, considerably more time will need to be spent on the training ground getting a zonal defense correct. However good the drills we use, practice, practice, practice is the key to success. This inevitably takes valuable, and limited, coaching time away from other areas of the game.

Further, since zonal marking is player intensive, with virtually every player having a role, it is something that needs working on with the whole team, and not just those players allocated to a man marking role.

Twenty (Drill): Zonal marking from corners:

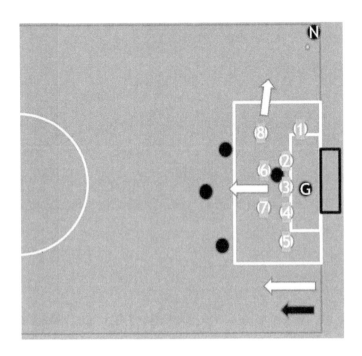

Players 1-5 are the normal zonal positions – teams will often line up with two players covering the central area – a sort of 3a and 3b.

Player 1) covers the under-hit cross to the near post. This will generally be a tall player;

Player 2) covers the near post;

Players 3) cover the central area. These will be the best headers of a ball;

Players 4 and 5) cover the far post, and the late run outside the far post;

Players 6-8 complete the defensive line up. 8 covers the pull back and moves out in case of a short corner; 6 covers the penalty spot and helps to clog up the central area making it harder for runs to be made. As with 3, there may be a couple of players employed here. 7 takes charge of the overhit cross.

Simply drill with lots of practice corners. When the defense wins the ball, and it is cleared (black arrow) they move out as a unit (white arrow) to catch their opponents offside from the second ball.

Twenty-One (Drill): Zonal marking from free kicks:

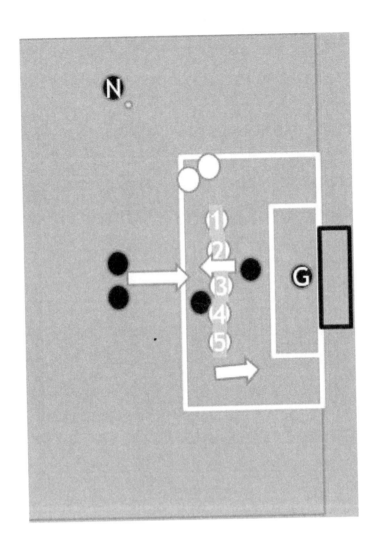

We should practice by holding free kicks from different positions. The most advanced black player is offside and should be ignored. He is likely to move backwards as the kick is taken, or not attempt to play the ball. The other attackers will seek to run into the space between the defensive line and the keeper. The defensive line moves back towards their own line to cover these runs.

The key points from this chapter are:

- Both zonal marking and man marking have their strengths and weaknesses;
- Man marking still has a place in the modern game, even though it might be presented as 'Neanderthal';
- Zonal marking requires more drill time, although both must be practised;
- Our conclusion is that a good defense employs both; a zonal system is used, with the opponent's most dangerous players also man marked;
- In terms of man marking in open play; it is quite an outmoded approach since it –
  - Does not always work;
  - Puts pressure on the marker, and can result in yellow and red cards;
  - If used, is best applied on a zonal basis, with different markers taking responsibility in different areas of the pitch;

- The 'nearest player' approach has its advocates, but can leave other gaps in the defense;
- Overall, we would not advocate its use in open play.

Let us now focus specifically on set piece defending, building on the suggestion above to combine a zonal approach with some man marking.

A Short message from the Author:

Hey, are you enjoying the book? I'd love to hear your thoughts!

Many readers do not know how hard reviews are to come by, and how much they help an author.

I would be incredibly thankful if you could take just 60 seconds to write a brief review on Amazon, even if it's just a few sentences!

Please head to the product page, and leave a review as shown below.

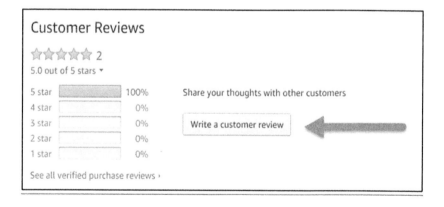

Thank you for taking the time to share your thoughts!

Your review will genuinely make a difference for me and help gain exposure for my work.

Organizing A Team for Set Piece Defending

We will look at five specific dead ball situations which might lead to a goal being conceded. These are corners, throw ins, indirect free kicks, direct free kicks and penalties.

Corners

Crowds become inadvertently excited when a corner is awarded to their team, and extra nervous when one is conceded. They shouldn't. They really are a very limited threat to a team. Conversion rates are extremely low; on average, in the professional game, around two to three goals are scored from everyone hundred corners.

But maybe that is because teams are well set up to deal with them. A number of questions face the coach when setting up their side to deal with corners:

1) Zonal, man marking, or a combination (hybrid) defense?
2) Should a player be left on each post? This really splits coaches. The argument for such a move is that these players

can clear the ball from the line. Against this are two arguments: Firstly, this takes players away from zonal defending or man marking, reducing any numerical advantage the defense enjoys when it comes to winning the first header; second, offside is taken from the equation. Of course, if the ball is headed directly into the goal, offside is in any case taken out of the equation, but actually most goals will come from a second or later touch in the box. Some coaches sit on the fence by using a player on one post (usually, the near one to help protect against the near post flick on.)

3) How many players to commit to defense? A good guide is to match the attackers in the box plus three, if that is possible.

4) How to deal with the short corner? Usually, one player will be positioned to cut out the near post corner. This player can then be used to rush out against a short corner. A defender covering the outside corner of the box (for the pulled back corner) also moves in to ensure that the offense does not gain a 2 v 1 advantage.

Twenty-Two (Tactic): Suggested line up for defending a corner.

The diagram below shows a good defensive plan for dealing with a corner. Using this as a basic organisation, players can adapt to the needs of each particular situation.

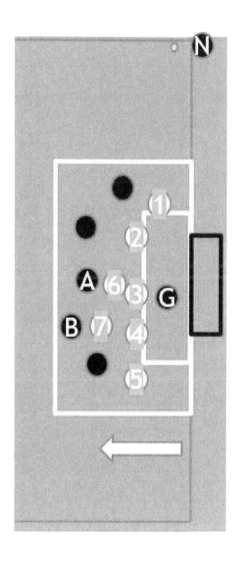

Here, attackers A and B are identified as strong headers of the ball, and are man marked. The remaining defenders mark zonally.

If the corner is played in long, and headed out of the box, once more players push forward to set an offside line.

Twenty-Three (Tactics): Defending the near post corner

Offensive sides will attempt to gain space from a corner by changing the way they set up, so the defense should be wary of changes of offensive line up. When a near post corner comes in, using the standard diagram above, the defense drops towards the goal line. Player 3 protects the goalkeeper by guarding the space in front of him to give him or her room to reach the ball. Player 2 can drop onto the near post if no player is there. If so, player 6 drops into the gap between 2 and 3. Player 5 tucks in towards the far post,

Twenty-Four (Tactics): Defending the deep corner

Again, we will use the diagram in drill twenty-two to highlight the tactical movement.

Once he realises the ball is hit long, player one tucks in, covering the near post. The remaining players shuffle across. Players 7, 4 and 5 seek to win the ball, while other players are there for the second ball. If the support is sufficient, players 3 or 4 drop to cover the far post on the line.

If it is an out swinging far post corner, the defense moves up, one on the six-yard box or closer to the keeper means they hold or move backwards in terms of forward/backwards movement.

Twenty-Five (Drill): Defending the pulled back corner

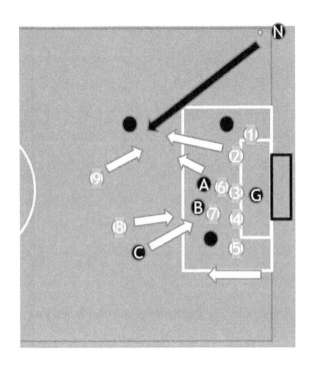

The pullback corner requires quick reactions from the defense. The nearest players close the ball – at least two – here marked by 6, 2 and 9. The defense, zonal and man marking, push out. The defense moves from a corner set up to one similar to a free kick. It is likely that either a shot, or a cross to a player running from deep will follow. Here we have marked this player with C. A player positioned for the breakout needs to be alive to this to track the run, as it will be difficult for a player rushing out to achieve the cover.

Drill with practice from various angles so that the defense become familiar with working as a unit and communicating.

Twenty-Six (Drill): Defending the short corner

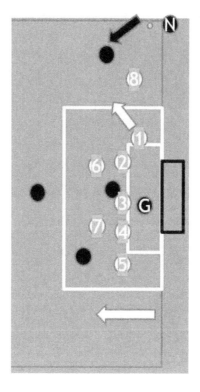

Player 1 becomes redundant if the ball is moved more deeply, so moves out to assist player 8. The defensive line moves out with the ball to play offside,

Throw In

Of all the defensive set plays, dealing with throw ins is probably easiest. The ball will arrive more slowly than from a pass played with the foot; it is possible to determine the trajectory since the ball will travel in the direction of the run up; even more rarely than with corners do goals result from throw ins.

Twenty-Seven (Technique): Dealing with the standard throw in

Stand a metre away from the target player so that he looks open. As the ball is thrown in, step neatly around the recipient, intercepting the ball. If this proves impossible, simply jockey the player to force him to lay off the pass back to the thrower.

Further, the defense aims to deny space to the opposition. Players cover the throw in range forcing the team to throw either backwards, or forwards down the line. A throw down the line is hard to control for the offense, and even if the defense fails to win the first ball, they are likely to win the second.

Twenty-Eight (Drill): Defending the throw in

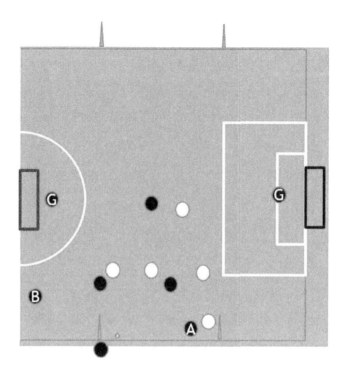

This drill features a six a side game on half a pitch where every restart is a throw in. Attacking restarts are from the more advanced cones, defensive ones from the deeper cone.

As can be seen, white defense has lined up so that all players are covered. The only options are back to B, or down the line to A. A throw to A is likely to result in lost possession since the white support will pick up any flick on.

With so many throw ins during a realistic match situation player will become used to getting into position quickly.

The drill can be extended to 11 a side on full length pitch.

The Long Throw

Some teams employ the long throw as an offensive weapon. The aim is to get a flick off a tall striker or even a defender. The ball is usually thrown into an area where the goalkeeper will come to try to reach the ball, but the crowd of players (offensive and defensive) makes this difficult and the ball may fall loose, with the keeper out of position.

Goals from long throw ins are messy, and certainly not for the purists. Still, they count as much as a thirty-yard screamer into the top corner, so defending them should not be completely dismissed.

There are two key aims in defending a long throw: sandwich the target man (one defender in front, one behind) and protect the keeper.

Twenty-Nine (Tactic and Drill): Defending the long throw

One player goes in front of the target man; another behind. A player (P) protects the keeper making sure that they have the space to come for the ball. Other defenders are there to pick up the loose ball.

A long throw seeks a flick on. It is very rare that the first header will have the power or angle to be headed into the net. Since the target is likely to be very obvious, this player should be man marked while other defense is located zonally.

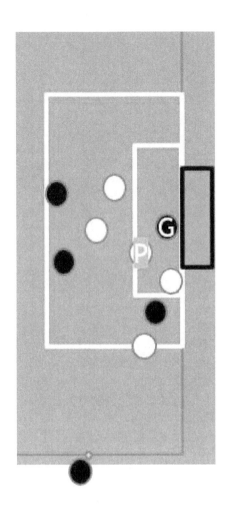

Free Kicks

From wide positions, there is little difference to defending a direct or indirect free kick. When a direct shot on goal is a possibility, the wall becomes a little more important and the charge down a little less. However, broadly, we can treat both types of free kick in the same way.

How to set a wall

The keeper is responsible for the wall. He or she will aim to protect one side of the goal, positioning the wall so that she can still see the ball.

Thirty (Tactic): Positioning a wall

1) Line up the outside player in a direct line between the ball and the near post. This player is key, so he should start facing the keeper to make communication easier;

2) Communicate how many players to be in the wall. Teams used to playing together will know the keeper's wishes in this respect depending on the location of the free kick;

3) For indirect or wide free kicks, use two or three players. Four or five might be employed for a straightish free kick within shooting range. However, too many players will obstruct the keeper's view;

71

4) Line up the rest of the wall against the first player;

5) If the keeper is worried about the ball being swerved around the wall, the first player may be moved a metre outside the near post;

6) When the wall is set, the first player turns, and the wall stands tightly shoulder to shoulder;

7) To jump or not to jump? Generally, most players will aim to lift free kicks over the wall, getting the ball to dip and swerve on its way to its target. Jumping does create the risk of a driven shot under the wall, but statistically it is a risk worth taking.

Thirty-One (Technical Point): Law change

The laws of the game changed for the 2019-20 season stopping attacking players from joining a wall. However, they have also been tightened on using arms to 'make the body larger'; hands need to be kept down or a penalty is risked.

Thirty-Two (Drill): Setting the wall

The cones in diagrams represent the recommended size of a wall for direct free kicks in the relevant position, with the number of players required identified by the number within the cone.

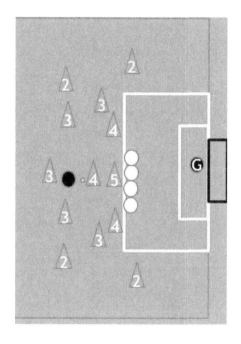

We can use the same guidance diagram to help keepers set their wall. Generally, strikers and midfielders are used in walls, the taller players towards the outside. One or two players are used to charge down the ball.

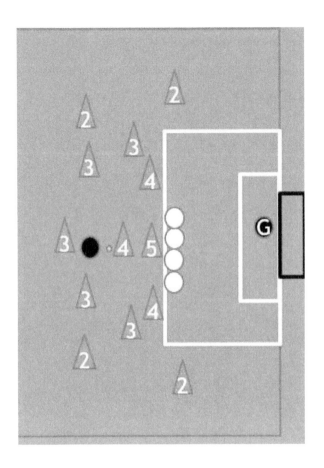

While goalkeepers will choose their own numbers for walls, the diagram above gives a guide as to a good size of wall for each position of the free kick. One or two maximum players should be used for an indirect free kick, plus one player to charge the shot

Try setting free kicks from different positions to help train the keeper and his wall to get into position quickly. One or two players (not shown above) should be allocated to charge down any free kick. This will discourage teams from changing the angle of a kick with a short pass, taking out the impact of the wall.

Positional Defending

The defensive line for a free kick is a judgement between the amount of space to be left behind the line and the area the keeper can dominate. Usually, the line will set either in line with the ball, or between the edge of the box and twenty-five yards out (for a free kick likely to result in a direct attempt on goal, or an attempt from a second player).

Many attacking teams now leave a player in an offside position. This player retreats as the ball is played, while one or two other players attack from deep aiming to break the line and attack the space behind it. It is therefore important to have runners to track and cover these movement.

Thirty-Three (Tactic): Setting up for defending free kicks

The following diagram demonstrates ideal positions for defending attacking free kicks. Drills should be used with the kick taken from a variety of positions, the players adjusting to the location of the ball.

As the free kick gets closer to the by-line, so the defensive shape becomes more as it would be if defending a corner.

Penalties

A chance for the keeper to be a hero! The psychology of penalty stopping is interesting. It is the only incidence in soccer when the likelihood of scoring outweighs that of missing. That shifts pressure from the keeper to the attacker and gives the keeper an advantage...if they can exploit it.

At the professional level, club staff prepare extensive dossiers on the likely penalty takers from opposing teams. The keeper has a fair idea of the penalty taker's favoured side, run up and technique. Find clips of the 2018 World Cup shootout between Colombia and England; the English keeper, Jordan Pickford, can be seen heading to his water flask before each penalty he faced. In fact, notes had been stuck to the flask, with information about each player. England won the shootout.

We are not suggesting that knowing about our opponents makes penalty stopping easier, but it shifts the balance of power very slightly in the direction of the keeper. Along with other techniques, this can turn the chances of saving the penalty more towards the keeper.

However, for most readers of this manual, the idea of giving our keepers a detailed breakdown of the penalty taker's technique is an impossibility. Therefore, we need to find as many other techniques as possible to give the keeper the advantage. The odds remain on the striker – about 80% of penalties are converted on average; but stopping one is as good as scoring at the other end. As such, it is a skill which needs to be practised.

Thirty-Four (Technique): Facing penalties

Each of the following can be employed by keepers to increase their chances of saving the ball or forcing a miss. Keepers will already use many of them, but there may be some ideas here which are worth adding to the goalkeeping arsenal.

1) Always remember that psychologically the pressure is on the attacker – do everything possible to increase that pressure;

2) Be the last to be ready; the more time the striker has to think, the less decisive he or she is likely to be;

3) Jump on the line, and make small sideways movements as the striker begins his run up; any distraction runs in the keeper's favour;

4) Give the striker the eyes, hinting the way we will be diving; we do not have to follow this, or we can. The point is that keeper can become the dominant one in the move, rather than the striker is we put doubt into his mind;

5) Wave arms up and down, clapping them above the head and dropping them to our knees in the run up; this is not only a distraction, but can make the goal seem smaller;

6) When diving, move forwards as well as sideways; a perfect penalty will always go in, but the further forward we can move, the lesser the angle in which the striker can score;

7) A surprisingly high number of penalties are hit straight; sometimes, delaying the dive can be successful as we are more likely to stop a poorly hit shot by delaying very slightly since we are not already committed to our dive.

8) Have a penalty saving session at least once a week; strikers love taking penalties. Try to get them to vary their run ups so that we have the chance to face different kinds of penalty – left foot, right foot, long run up, straight run up, angled run, delayed run up, short run up, pause in run and so forth.

In this chapter we have covered defensive tactics and shape for set pieces. As with other defensive patterns, drills and practice are key to keeping them tight. Some, such as zonal marking, require extensive drilling and great spatial awareness; others, such as man marking, need good concentration.

All, however, involve the whole team.

Once more, it can be said enough that defense in a whole team responsibility, not just that of the back four and keeper.

The next chapter will take a slightly different form. We will offer a number of diagrams highlighting the main defensive shapes and set ups for both being out of position, and during transition.

Defensive Shape

The following is an extensive list of the formations most commonly employed in soccer. We cannot say that one is better than another. If it were, then all teams would use it. However, like fashion, trends come and go. Rarely is the sweeper used in the modern game, but it seems a reasonable assumption that at some point in the next twenty years it will fall back into fashion.

One thing to note, and it is a good thing, is that tighter rules on foul play and better pitches have led to the game producing defenders with much greater technical ability. What starts in the professional side of the sport, soon spreads down to the amateur and youth elements.

That we have nowadays ball playing defenders, and very few who see their role as simply kicking anything that moves. That is reflected in the shapes and formations we have highlighted below. For each, we have outlined three points: the strengths and weakness of the formation, plus the characteristics of players needed to make effective use of it. We have also identified close variations of the system.

We have included for each a tactical clue to employing the system, and a key technique required by players to deliver it, plus a drill for them to practise this technique.

Thirty-Five (Formation): 4-4-2

Strengths: This is a common structure with which players will be familiar. It is simple to use, with the defense simply dropping to two banks of four when possession is lost. The two strikers are available to receive a pass during transition and can also drop back to pressure the opposition. The flat back line makes offside relatively easy to play.

Weaknesses: The system is effective defensively, but ineffective when the ball is won since it is very narrow. The wide midfielders have to tuck in to deny space when out of possession or the ball is easily played through them. If players do get in behind the flat back four, the system is weak.

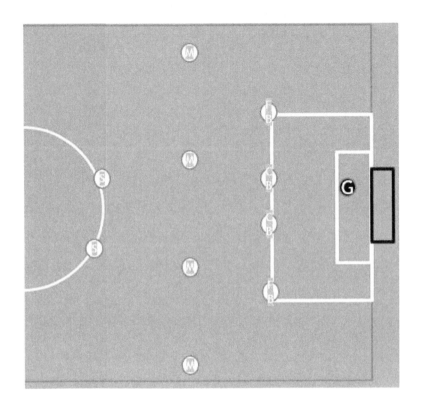

Thirty-Six (Tactic):

For the system to be at its best defensively it is important to stop opposing players from operating 'between the lines'. This is the area between the line of midfield four and defensive four. Number 10s in particular like to get into this space and find the time to make killer passes in behind the back four.

A tactic which can be employed to stop this is to drop one of the strikers back into the midfield four and slip a defensive central midfielder between the lines to track the runs of the number 10. Thus, the system switches from 4-4-2 to 4-1-4-1.

Secondly, the system is prone to allowing number 8s, attacking midfielders, from breaking late through the lines. Tactically, the central midfield must be aware of this risk, and focus on tracking such runs. We will focus on this in the next section.

Thirty-Seven (Technique): Tracking runs from central midfield:

In the old days, tracking would be a 1 on 1 man marking system. Players had less freedom to break out of position, so it was simpler to identify runners. The game today is more fluid, and therefore the coach should set up his or her team with each midfielder responsible for a zone. When a player breaks through that zone, they track them.

However, even this is too rigid to be effective in a 4-4-2 set up, since midfielders will make dummy runs to create space by taking out a defensive midfielder. Therefore, players track opponents who break through the zone that they are in, and the two strikers are aware of what is developing and slot into the midfield space left by their teammate.

Thirty-Eight (Drill):

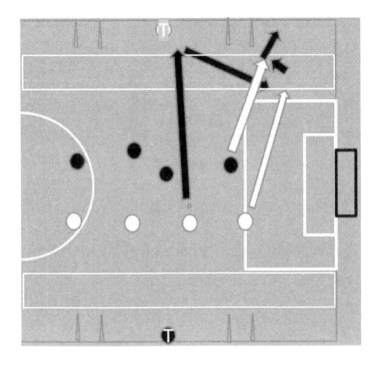

We like this drill to help players learn to track their opponents. Each side has five players. One is the target man, who cannot score, and cannot be tackled. There are then four midfielders from each team who operate as offensive runners when in position, and trackers when not in possession.

Players can score in either of their goals, and play develops as follows. Each play must include a pass to the target man, who lays off

84

a pass to a runner. The runner then tries to break away from his tracker to score into the open goal. Provide the target man is used once in each play, there can be as many other passes as required within the time. Players can only score in the scoring zone. Plays end when possession changes, the ball goes dead or twenty seconds passes.

Thirty-Nine (Formation): 4-3-3

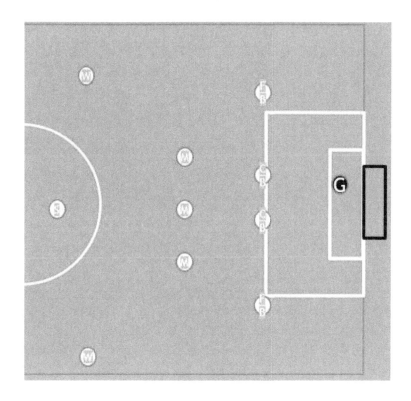

This shape is very popular at the moment, and it is easy to see why. It is more threatening than the 4-4-2 on transition, with wide players able to exploit space left by marauding full backs. However, this book is about defense, and it is also a very effective defensive shape when possession is lost.

The major weakness of the system is that the midfield can be too narrow. The wingers or full backs are required to support in wide positions, which can leave gaps elsewhere,

Forty (Tactic):

For the system to work defensively, a lot of pressure is placed on the front three players. The two wide men drop to make a midfield five, while the central striker harries any attack built from the centre of the park.

As can be imagined, a high level of fitness is required from these players, who will need to cover a lot of ground.

Forty-One (Technique): Pressing from the front

This press, similar to the high press but used as a second stage if the high press has been bypassed, is effective defensively. Again, it requires high levels of fitness from the attack and midfield. The fundamental unit shifts to four at the back and a midfield four who are fluid.

The fourth midfielder is made up of one of the front three who is not pressing the ball. The other two of the front three work as a pair to pressure the man on the ball and force a pass. When the pass is made, it is likely to be lateral since there will be little space for a forward pass. Then, the nearest striker, plus the one of the now midfield four, move out to harry, and the spare striker drops in to renew the midfield four.

The technique for this pressure is to provoke an error from the opposition rather than actively seek to win the ball with a tackle. Therefore, the pressure is applied by one player rushing to the ball, but standing off a metre, sideways to the ball, denying the player in possession space to pass or run.

The second pressuring player gives five or so metres but positions themselves where the pass is likely to be made. Thus, when an error is forced, they are in a position to intercept.

ill):

The _ alf pitch is divided into three zones, with four players in each. The aim is for the teams at either end to play the ball through the middle zone to the other end. The players in the central zone must aim to prevent this by kicking the ball out, winning possession, intercepting the pass or forcing their opponents to play the ball out.

Two defense players are permitted in the zone where the ball is being played. These may rotate as the ball is played across the zone.

When the defense succeed in their goal, they swap with the side who have just lost the ball.

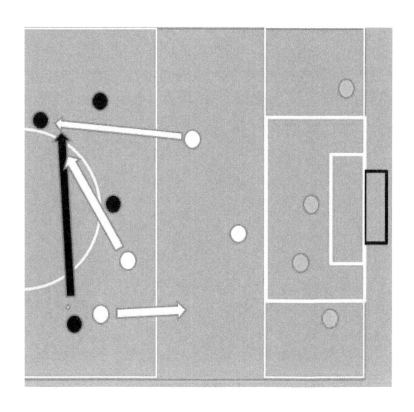

Forty-Three (Formation): 5-3-2

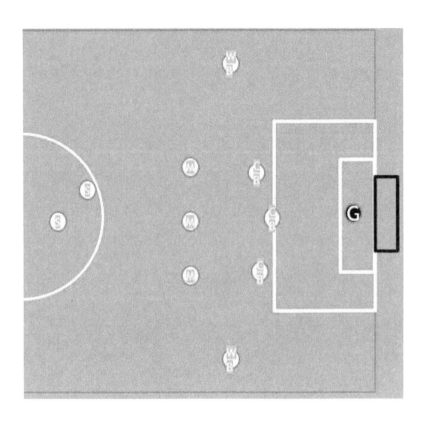

Although it may seem defensive, with five at the back, 5-3-2 is actually quite an offensive formation. The wing backs get forward a lot, turning the system into a 3-5-2. The unfashionable but recently promoted Premier League team, Sheffield United, have taken it a step further offensively. They employ the wide central defenders as overlapping full backs when on the attack, with midfielders covering.

Defensively it is solid, and the extra centre back allows security to be maintained at the back. Under this system, one of the centre backs is expected to be comfortable enough on the ball to dribble into midfield, where it is possible to be over run.

Forty-Four (Tactic):

A risk with this system is that a skilful and pacy team can catch it out on the break. With full backs pushed on, the midfield committed to attack and one of the centre backs helping out, it is a frightening offensive prospect.

However, on transition, teams may push a fast player wide into the space left by the wing backs. This means one of the centre backs must come out, and they could be exposed for pace. Further, a lot of room is left in the centre, with just one defense player left to cope 1 v 1 with a striker.

This is countered by tactical discipline by the three central midfielders, one of who must sit to protect the back two. This player will then be the one drawn wide defending the break. Good communication and firm positional discipline are essential not to have the formation exposed.

Forty-Five (Technique):

91

An important technique for wing backs, who are likely to be chasing towards their own goal, is the ability to poke tackle. We looked very briefly at this in the section on sliding tackles.

The technique for the poke tackle is get alongside the runner. The tackler leans into the opponent, shoulder to shoulder, attempting to break their balance on the ball. At the same time, the outside leg is extended, knee bent and studs downwards.

The aim is to 'poke' the ball away from the runner, and out of play (in most scenarios for a wing back). The restart gives the team a chance to re-organize defensively.

Forty-Six (Drill):

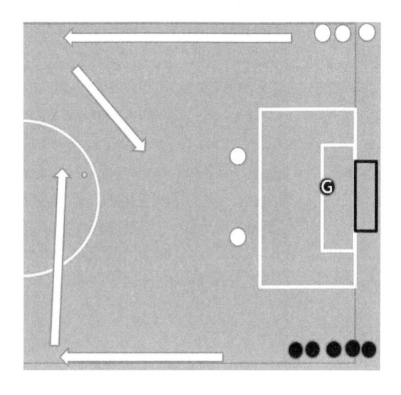

Since this formation is one which often breaks up in shape at transition, the drill above is a good one for practising getting into position. It can be used with anything up to full 11 v 11. However, our 6 a side version (including keeper) is a good number for the half pitch drill. The black team sprint from the corner flag to the halfway line, collect the ball and build an attack. The white team have two defenders and a keeper in place, but the remainders sprint from the opposite corner flag and must then chase back and get into position. They cannot touch the ball until the blacks have played the ball.

Forty-Seven (Formation): Midfield Diamond Formation

The midfield diamond is a variation on 4-4-2. It is a strong defensive shape in transition since the deepest midfield player sits, and when winning the ball players can advance quickly. However, as can easily be seen, it is a shape that leaves gaps in central midfield (to counter this, coaches pull the wide players in tights, denying space in the centre but leaving the side open to a switch in play). As such, it is vulnerable to a determined attack, and usually will shift back to a standard 4-4-2 or even 4-5-1 when under pressure.

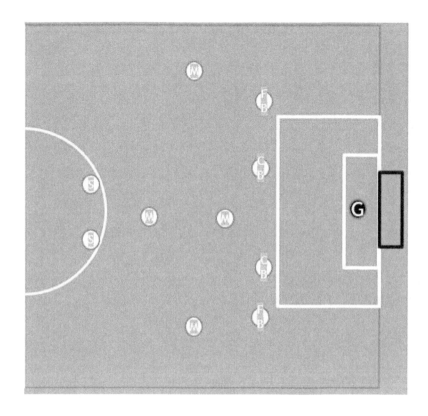

Forty-Eight (Tactic):

The system can be effective when dealing with teams who like to press an offensive player between the midfield and defensive lines. By switching one of the two strikers plus the advanced midfielder into the midfield four, the defensive midfielder is naturally situated between the lines to close down a number 10 who tries to operate in this space.

Forty-Nine (Technique): Playing offside:

A well-executed offside trap is an effective weapon. However, it needs plenty of practice to get it running smoothly. The defense moves forward as a unit a moment before the pass is played, catching the striker or runner offside. The call to move forward often lies with a full back, who from their wide position, can see across the line.

Trust to follow the call is needed. The player making the call will look for two factors:

1) A player making a run;
2) The passer putting their head down (usually a sign the pass is coming)

Fifty (Drill): Playing offside

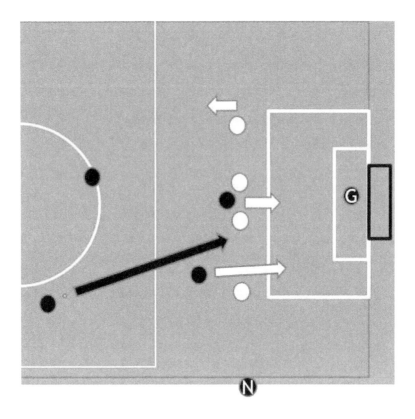

The offense has two passers, a runner and a striker. The defense may not enter the top half of the practice pitch. One of the passers makes their delivery either to the striker or the runner, and the defense try to catch the player offside. The player marked N in the drill acts as a linesman (referee's assistant) to judge whether the defense have worked effectively.

It is worth noting that the offside trap has a flaw at amateur level, in that referee's assistants may not be used to this complex role, and may miss the most highly attuned offside traps, rendering them not only useless, but an actual danger to the defense, since the offside but unidentified striker will be through on goal!

Fifty-One (Formation): Sweeper System

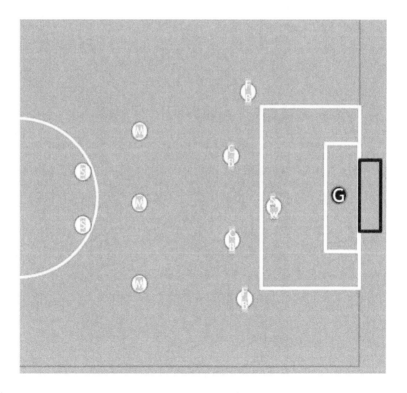

It is fair to say that the sweeper system is out of fashion at the moment. It is vulnerable to wide breaks and is hard to use in an offside trap.

However, used well it provides the offensive advantage of having a player comfortable with bringing the ball out of defense and starting an attack. Defensively, it means that cover is always available.

Fifty-Two (Tactic):

The sweeper system promotes control. The defense should dictate the pace of play, with the sweeper bringing the ball out from the back. Therefore, this player needs a number of attributes: a great reading of the game so that they can be correctly positioned; self-discipline in not committing to the tackle unless sure of success or a last resort; skilled passing and good dribbling skills. The style lends itself to regular long balls – not hit and hope or down the channels, but cross field switches of play, and balls out wide.

Fifty-Three (Technique):

There are many techniques required of the sweeper. The diagonal pass is one of the most important. The pass should be hit with the instep; the player leans back slightly to get lift. He striker through the ball, twisting the hips in the direction of travel, and swinging the arms to generate momentum and balance. He strikes the ball at the bottom.

Fifty-Four (Drill):

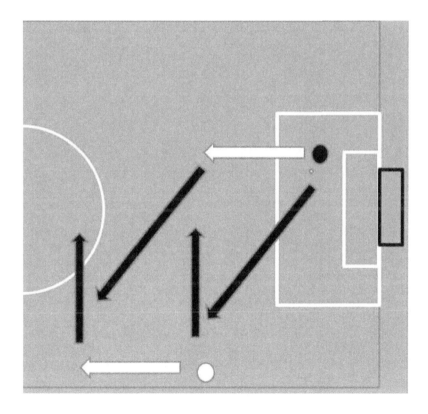

This drill can work the length of the pitch. The passer (sweeper) takes a touch before passing.

Fifty-Five (Formation): 4-2-3-1

This is a strong line up, with plenty of defensive support allowing the front four the freedom to get forward without too many defensive traits. On the downside, much responsibility is placed on the two deeper midfielders, the central defensive midfielders. These must be supremely fit, able on the ball, able to find a pass but also protect the back four.

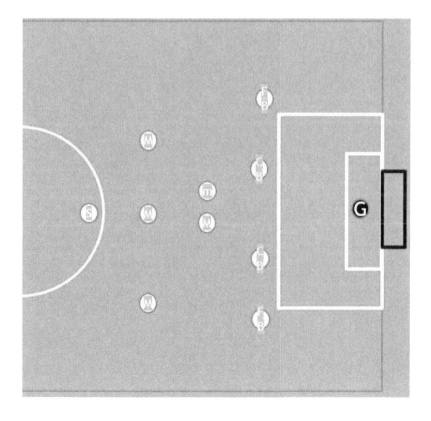

Fifty-Six (Tactic):

Defensively, the wide attacking midfielders track back and the full backs push forward to deny space. The shape then becomes a 2-4-3-1. The space is in the channels wide, but because the centre of the park is crowded, it is hard for midfielders to find passes into this zone. If a central defender is pulled out of position for a pass into the channel, a full back of central defensive midfielder drops into the back line.

Fifty-Seven (Technique):

The central defensive midfielder (CDM) is the link player. He or she needs to constantly aware of what is happening, both in terms of who is on the ball for their team, and who to pass to when the ball comes. At the same time, the player is keeping their eye out for danger. They should therefore always be sideways on to the ball, so that they can cover the widest visual arc possible.

: Central defensive midfielder

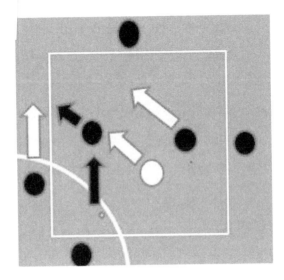

The aim of the drill is for the white player to press the ball in the grid forcing the black player to pass the ball out of the grid, rather than to his teammate in the grid. This is a tiring drill, so the CDM changes regularly.

Fifty-Nine (Formation): 4-1-4-1

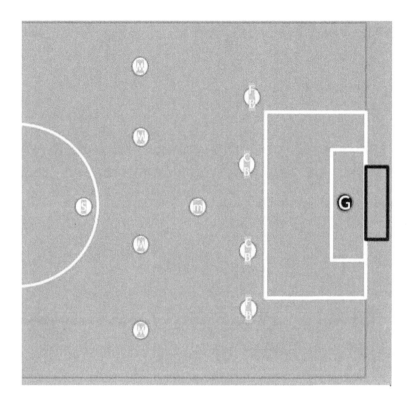

A strong formation defensively, perhaps the strongest (although it is less effective as an attacking strategy since the lone striker can become isolated. Indeed, this leads to its main defensive weakness, that it is hard to play out and therefore the formation can induce a lot of pressure).

However, the set-up is designed to withstand pressure, and if the wide midfielders have the pace to get forward quickly, the formation can be good for playing on the break.

Sixty (Tactic):

The single CDM man marks players who shift into the space between the lines. The back four squeeze up to further limit the amount of space available in this crucial area.

Sixty-One (Technique):

As important as defense is, if this is the only aspect of the game then a team will never score, and therefore never win. Since this formation lends itself to attacking quickly at transition, we can examine the technique for doing this.

When the ball is won, the two wide midfielders break forward. The two central advanced midfielders show for the ball, and the central striker drops a little. The aim is to either hit the pass long into the wide, open channels and draw a central defender out, or play through the central striker to get the ball wide.

Sixty-Two (Drill):

The deep midfielder begins with the ball and has three passing options. The two central defenders are overwhelmed on the break.

Simply play the drill several times, working on timing of runs to stay onside and weight of pass to lead to a goalscoring chance.

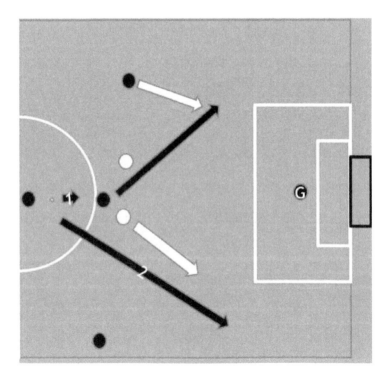

Sixty-Three (Formation): 4-3-2-1 – The Christmas Tree:

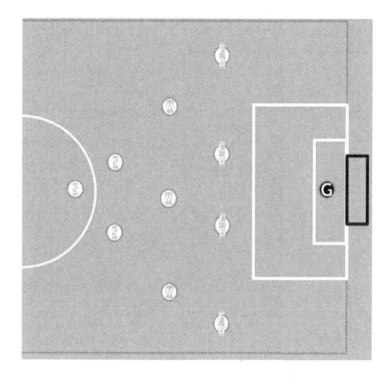

The Christmas Tree enjoyed a short spell of popularity in the 1990s. As can be seen, it is a compact defensive unit which is difficult to break down for an opposition. However, its limitations are equally clear in the offensive sense. The main problem with the system was that in order to flood forward at transition, the shape was itself broken up – full backs in particular needed to get forward and wide to create space.

If attacks break down, the system is then vulnerable to the counterattack.

Sixty-Four (Tactic):

The back seven try to hold their shape, with the front three pressing the ball. The midfield three drift left to right and back again with play.

Sixty-Five (Technique):

Because the defense is packed, this sort of system leads opposing sides to look to cross from deep. This means that the defense is running back while the strikers are running onto the ball. The technique for central defenders is to get chest on to the cross as quickly as possible in order to be able to head away. They then need to change direction and move out in order to catch any strikers offside from a second pass into the box.

Sixty-Six (Drill):

Two cones mark a starting line for strikers and defenders. The ball is played in from wide. The attackers run on to the ball in an attempt to win the header. The defence moves back towards goal, and attempt to win the aerial battle. They must then move out as a unit to catch any strikers offside should the ball come back into the penalty area.

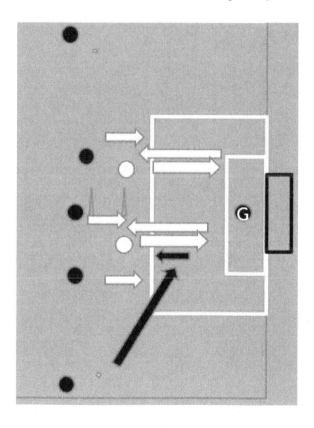

The drill can be operated with or without a goalkeeper. With a keeper makes it more challenging for the offense; without, it is harder for the defense.

Sixty-Seven (Formation): The False Nine

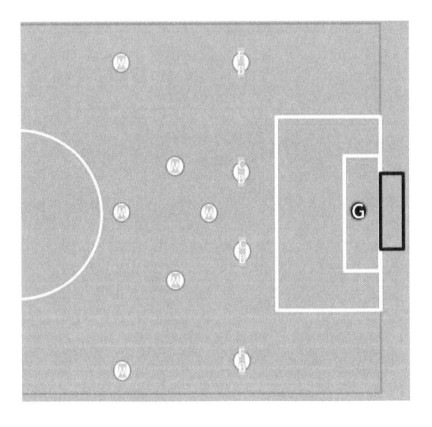

The great Spanish team of the mid 2000s and into the early 2010s developed the false nine, a system without a dedicated striker. With such outstanding midfield talent as Iniesta, Xavi and Fabregas, and (following the injury to Fernando Torres) no absolutely world class central striker, they adopted the system.

Although it seems a defensive set up, with the extra midfielder, in fact it is very aggressive, with players having the freedom and fluidity interchange positions and get into central striking roles.

Its defense was built on the fact that the Spanish dominated possession with their tiki-taka football, full of short, controlled passing. However, the back four was solid.

Other teams have tried the system – notably Chelsea in the Premier League in the mid to late 2010s – but with only marginal success.

Sixty-Eight (Tactic):

Since this is an attacking formation, the defensive tactics are as for a standard back four. The defense settles into a 4-6 formation when the ball is lost, denying space to the opposition. It breaks quickly on its own transition.

Sixty-Nine (Technique):

There are no specific defensive techniques we have not covered already. Thus, any of those covered already can be employed. The main technical issue is that, because offensively the system is fluid, so it must be defensively. Therefore, it is important that every player knows both their job…and how to deliver it!

Seventy (Drill):

Use a full pitch and 11 v 11. One side (white) sets up normally, the other (black) retains an advanced back four, one CDM and the remaining players stand in their attacking penalty area. The play starts from level with the corner of the defensive penalty box and plays out normally. The blacks have the ball. The white team must regain their defensive shape as quickly as possible, with the back five holding up play long enough for this to be achieved.

This drill can be adapted to get any formation used to regaining shape at transition.

The ideas we have emphasised in this chapter are:

- There are many formations and shapes that a coach can adopt;
- Fundamentally, in defense, these form into two lines, perhaps with an additional defender between them, that are hard to break down;
- The biggest risk to any defense is when it is out of shape at transition;
- Coaches should work hard with their team – the whole team – at regaining shape when the ball is lost.

NB – the easiest time to regain shape is when the ball is dead. Ironically, one of the best forms of defense is a shot. Since this will often result in the ball going dead, it gives the team a chance to regain their shape.

The greatest vulnerability is often when the ball is lost in possession in the attacking third, or when a team has pushed forward for a free kick or corner, and the ball is lost.

Three v Two Defending

Transition is a crucial part of the modern game. As teams have learned of the benefits of committing more and more players to attacking situations, so they leave themselves increasingly exposed to the counterattack when possession transitions.

The growth of pacy, technically gifted players with vision means that many top sides counterattack with speed and accuracy, placing extensive pressure on the defense. There are many, many examples of this in action to be found in online clips and watch any review of a round of fixtures in a top European league and goals resulting from transition proliferate. One fine example from the 2017-18 season came from the German Bundesliga.

In a thrilling match between Borussia Dortmund and FC Schalke, the latter are pressing hard when a slightly wayward pass is intercepted and played quickly upfield into the wide right-hand channel. The speedy striker Pierre Emerick Aubameyang pounces and with the defense stretched accelerates down the wing. He creates space and whips in a cross where Mario Götze is waiting to bury the simple chance with a powerful far post downwards header.

What becomes a trend in the professional game rapidly becomes a part of the amateur and youth system as coaches and players seek to emulate their role models.

Therefore, a situation occurs where the defense is outnumbered. Here are some methods to help defenses to cope with this situation. The focus is on the most common scenario, where the offense gains a three v two advantage, but the principles easily adapt to other numerical situations.

Seventy-One (Tactic): The fundamental tactics to apply when caught in a three v two situation

The aim is to slow down the attack until defensive reinforcements can arrive. In order to do this:

1) The defense tries to push the player with the ball wide and away from goal;

2) The closest defender moves towards the ball, but holds back from committing to the tackle unless a real loss of control from the striker occurs;

3) The defender must stay on their feet. If they go to ground, and are beaten, there is no time to recover and a three v one scenario, which we now have, is highly likely to result in a goal;

4) The second defender drops deep and centrally, placing themselves in the best position to move to the ball if a pass is played;

5) The player in the most dangerous position is the one on whom to keep the closest eye, while maintaining an awareness of the position of the third player;

6) The role of the goalkeeper is crucial; he or she communicates to assist their defense, shifting players to the ball or cover positions;

7) The keeper moves further off of their line to act as a sweeper should an overhit pass result. The keeper drops back slightly as the offense close in on goal.

Seventy-Two (Drill): Rondo drill:

One way to improve the capacity of our defense in a three v two situation is to create familiarity in training. The next few drills are based on the rondo technique. Any rondo drill involving two defenders works. Rondos are a system developed by Barcelona and now widely used across all levels of the game. The drill is characterised by a loading of players on one side. Whichever drill is being practised is worked on with just a small number of opposing players, for example, a five v two scenario.

The small amount of defense puts some pressure on those working on the skill or technique, but also allows them enough time to develop and hone the relevant aspect of the game they are practising. Development usually occurs by shrinking the amount of space in which the drill takes place.

As we stated earlier, defense drills are marked by the need for much repetition which can be time consuming. However, the crucial skills of communication and working together will be developed as a by-product of offense focussed rondo drills. Coaches can use pairs of defender to act as the opposition in rondo drills; while this will not specifically address three v two defending, it will help these players to work together and communicate better, skills which they can then apply more effectively in three v two situations.

Seventy-Three (Drill): Rondo drill

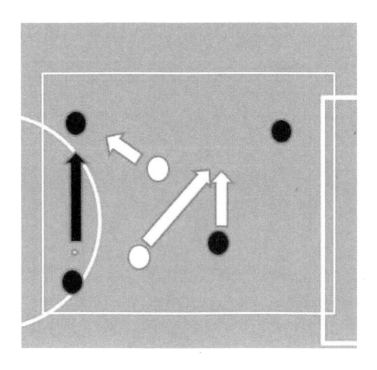

A very simple drill. The black team use their extra players to keep possession in the grid. They look to pass quickly, with the ball on the ground. The whites work together to make this as difficult as possible, slowing down the passing or forcing the blacks into an error.

Seventy-Four (Drill): Rondo drill

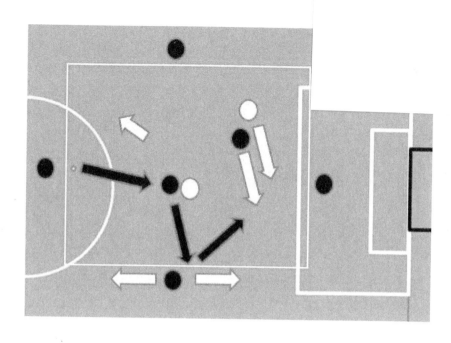

Two v Two in a grid, with the weighted team having a get out pass to one of the players on the outside. The whites have two aims – ideally to win the ball or force a mis-pass. Failing this, they try to deny the blacks in the grid space and get them to pass to the outside.

Seventy-Five (Drill): Rondo drill

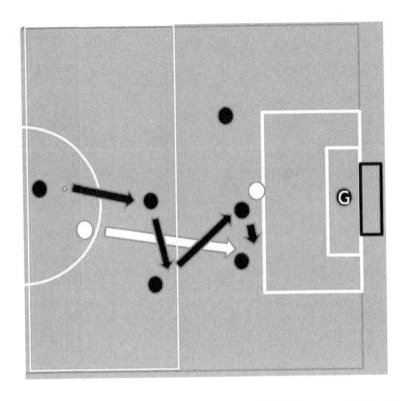

The practice area is divided into two. Each half starts with 3 v 1. The defense also has a goalkeeper. The white defender in the upfield grid may move into the defensive area once the ball is passed into it.

The deepest defender attempts to slow play long enough for his team mate to get back and offer support.

Seventy-Six (Drill): Rondo drill

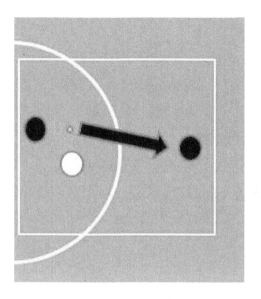

The simplest of all – and nothing wrong with that! Simple 2 v 1 in a grid, with the defense aiming to knock the ball out of the grid. The key is not to commit to the tackle unless control is lost, but to look to intercept the ball.

The black team have a two-touch limit to ensure that they keep playing the ball.

We will look now at some 3-2 match type scenarios. In each example, we have produced a diagram to illustrate the scenario, and also the movement and actions of the defense. These scenarios can be set up as drills, either on a half pitch, or using a grid.

Seventy-Seven (Drill and Technique): Three v Two focus on slowing down

The intention is the for the white defense to slow down the attack as far as possible. The defenders back off, sideways to the dribbling striker. They will make a tackle at the edge of the box, but not before. In a match situation, if they can slow down the attack enough, more defenders will get back to support.

Aim one is to force the dribbler to try and beat them, and win possession;

If this fails, they aim to force the dribbler to pass the ball wide where there is relatively less danger. Finally, they aim to pressure the shot to such an extent that the keeper can save, or the shot misses the target.

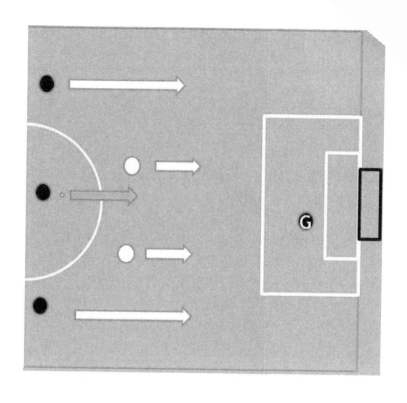

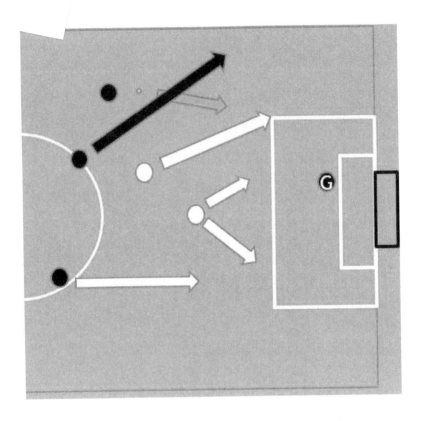

The defender nearest the ball moves across to cover the two players. On the principle that the further away from goal the ball, the greater the chance of an attacking coming to nothing, he positions his body to invite the pass wide. The deeper defender drops, sideways on, so he can cover either the pass to the opposite striker or become extra cover if the ball does go wide. Again, slowing down the opposition by not committing to the tackle unless absolutely necessary is the key aim.

Seventy-Nine (Drill and Technique): Three v Two focus on the goalkeeper

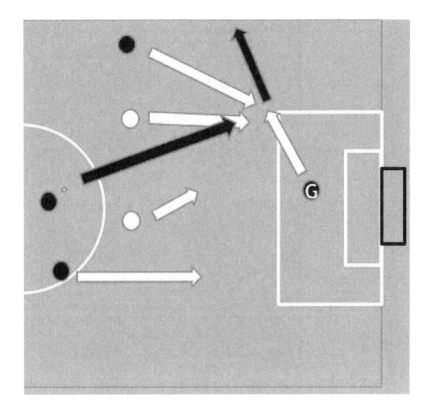

Note here the goalkeeper's advanced position as the break occurs. The diagonal ball inside the two defenders could be devastating, but the keeper is far enough advanced to sweep the ball to safety.

It is important that a keeper makes a decision and commits. Sometimes, the keeper will get it wrong (and it is important not to give away a foul, then, as that would almost certainly result in a red card), but often the pressure of a keeper rushing out is enough to put a striker off their intent, and force an error.

Being left in no man's land, when the keeper has half come for the ball, then changed their mind, is worst of all. Here, they are vulnerable to the early shot, or chip, as well as a straight dribble or lateral pass across an unguarded goal.

Note, when the keeper rushes out, the deepest defender heads to cover the goal line.

Eighty (Drill): Three v Two (1) – Developing Understanding

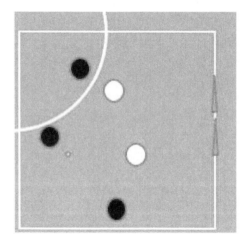

A simple drill using three v two, a grid and a small goal. There is no goalkeeper, which forces the defense to close down as tightly as possible. The strikers aim to score as many goals as they can in a given period. Each time the defense win the ball, intercept or force a shot wide, they score a point.

The defenders must focus on staying on their feet, communicating and keep close together to support.

Eighty-One (Drill): Three v Two (2)

This is a fast action variant on other 3 v 2 defense drills. Here, multiple players line up and rotate. The two defense players (whites) defend, using the skills and techniques developed. Then then rotate with the players on the cones after each round.

Similarly, the three strikers aim to score, using any techniques that they wish. They too rotate with the players on the cones after each round.

The drill is completed when one of the following occurs:

- A goal is scored;
- The keeper saves a shot;
- The ball goes out of play;
- The white defense wins the ball;
- The ball is knocked outside the width of the permitted attacking area. That is the area within the cones and the outside edge of the penalty box. Thus, it can be seen that the defense will aim to force the attack wide where there is

less direct danger, and more time (in a real match) for reinforcements to arrive.

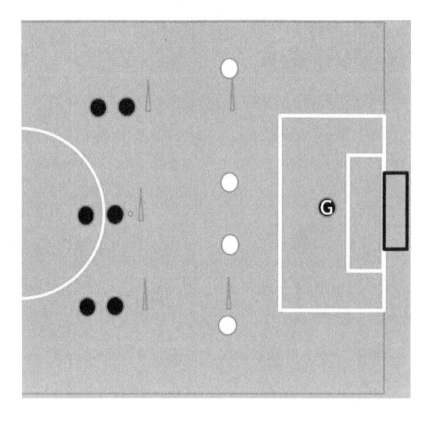

From this chapter we can take away the following key points:

- Being exposed to three v two, and other imbalances in offense v defense, is an inevitable consequence of the more attack orientated game soccer is becoming;
- Communication is crucial in dealing with these situations;

- Slowing down the pace of a counterattack is the key procedure to negate its danger.

In the next chapter we will spend some time looking at the role of the player between the posts.

The Importance of the Goalkeeper in Defense

When researching for this chapter, we found a coaching blog from 2010. It states that the purpose of the 'keeper is to keep the ball out of the net. Perhaps it is a sign of how quickly the game is changing in that top coaches would see a triple role for goalkeepers these days. Yes, he or she must be proficient at stopping the ball from entering the goal, but must also:

1) Have the ability to launch attacks;
2) Be a spare outfield player, a kind of old-fashioned sweeper.

For these two roles, the keeper must develop excellent touch, the ability to pass with accuracy, vision and two good feet. Today' person between the sticks should not neglect these aspects of their game. It raises the interesting philosophical question as to whether the better keeper is the one who can save well, but also be an effective player with his or her feet, or the best shot stopper.

The jury is out on that one.

However, this book is about developing defense. Therefore, we will concentrate on these aspects of their role.

Positioning

Where to stand? Let us start from the front, so to speak. Most readers will have seen the great long-distance goals scored by players who saw the keeper advanced and lofted a shot from fifty yards into the net. Indeed, 'Nayim, from the halfway line,' is still a chant sung by Tottenham Hotspur fans about their ex player who scored against their rivals, Arsenal, in a European Cup final in the last millennium.

Followers of English football will know that Tottenham Hotspur fans cling on to every little achievement, however obscure and tangential to their own team, having few of their own in the last fifty years!

Nevertheless, a modern keeper must take up an advanced position when his or her own team are on the attack. This is for a couple of reasons. As the deepest player, there will always be time for the keeper if he receives a back pass, since any striker will be in line with the defense to avoid offside. (There is no offside from a back pass, of course. However, a striker who hangs around the goalkeeper is out of the game in all other scenarios). Thus, the keeper is the spare player who can restart an attack if it breaks down.

More importantly, an advanced keeper can act as a sweeper to cut out long balls played when attack transitions into defense.

But although it is important that a keeper feels confident enough to advance up the pitch, her natural home is the penalty box. It is here that the goalie's biggest advantage, their hands, come into play.

Positioning in the box, and, for that matter, out of it, is a technical matter which can be taught. It relies on two fundamentals – firstly the bisector and secondly identifying landmarks to help co-ordinate positioning.

Eighty-Two (Technique): Using the bisector

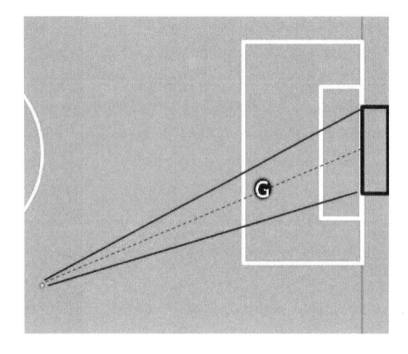

The bisector is found as follows: Imagine two lines between the ball and each of the posts, Then, imagine a line that splits these into two, and runs from the ball to the centre of the goal. This is the bisector.

As can clearly be seen in the above diagram, the further out that the keeper stands, the narrower the angle either side of the bisector in which a goal can be scored.

Eighty-Three (Technique): Finding landmarks

However, it is easy for players to lose their orientation as they are moving around. Coaches should encourage their keepers, even from a young age, to use other landmarks to help them to remain orientated. Learning to position correctly even from U7 levels will help keepers to develop good habits from the start.

Both on field and off field landmarks can be employed. On field landmarks can be found on every pitch and include:

- The penalty spot;
- The D at the edge of the box;
- The corners of the box;
- The centre spot;
- The opposing goal posts;
- Corner flags;
- Half-way flags;
- Something unique about the pitch on which the game is played, such as a centrally located muddy patch;
- A keeper's own goal posts (although using these as markers involves the keeper taking their eye of the

developing play, and so should only be used when the keeper is sure not shot is imminent.)

Off field landmarks vary from pitch to pitch. They might include:

- At higher levels, advertising hoardings which help give a keeper a marker as to how far advanced they are;
- A hat, or cone, placed mid-way between the edge of the box and the half-way line, which a keeper has put down to give them a sense of position;

On field markers tend to be better for the keeper to identify the position of her goal behind them, while off field markers help the keeper to determine how far out of their box they are standing.

Eighty-Four (Drill): Positioning

This is a very good goalkeeping drill to aid positioning and is much less complicated than the diagram below suggests.

The attacker with the ball dribbles at a defender. As the ball approaches the edge of the box the keeper (G) moves back along the line of the bisector to prepare for a shot and to reduce the chance of being chipped.

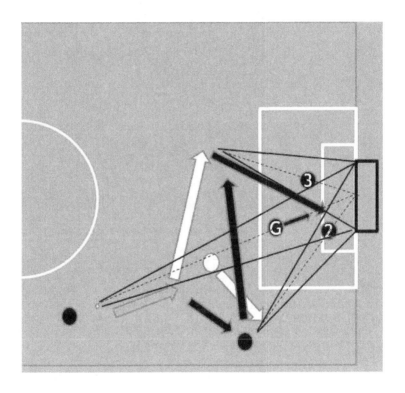

The dribbler at some stage passes wide and moves off to take up a more central position for the return. The defender covers the pass. The keeper (now marked 2) shifts along the new bisector, and heads back toward his goal. As the ball is wide, he now anticipates the likelihood of a cross and wants to be in a position where he can advance to catch the ball, and make sure it does not go over his head into a dangerous position.

The attacker can choose whether to dribble, cross, pass or shoot. In our example above he has passed. The goalkeeper now moves to the new bisector and takes up a position a little further advanced in his box to narrow the angles on a shot (3).

Play the drill many times, helping the keeper to get used to identifying the bisectors and deciding on how advanced their position on it will be. The coach can pause between rotations of the drill to discuss the keeper's positioning.

Shot Stopping

Positioning is important, since the bisector is the line which offers the best chance to save a shot. However, a keeper still needs to make the save. Good keepers not only have excellent positioning and, these days, very good feet, but coaches seeking to find the next Gordon Banks or Manuel Neuer should also look for the following characteristics:

- Concentration;

- Good reactions;

- Strong hands;

- Bravery;

- Mental strength – a midfielder's error might result in a lost ball, and a striker's a missed chance. A keeper error often leads to a goal!

Eighty-Five (Drill): Reactions

A simple warm up style drill. The coach stands with a number of balls. He throws to one side of the keeper, who dives, catches, returns the ball to the coach and gets back into position. The coach then throws the ball to the other side, and so forth. A new ball is used if the save is punched away, or the ball goes in the goal, so pace is maintained. After a while, the coach moves on to 'passing' the ball from side to side for the keeper to save.

Eighty-Six (Drill): One v One

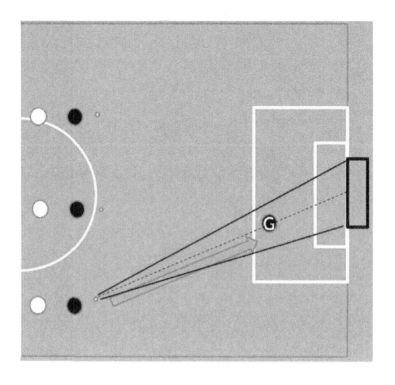

The striker runs at the keeper. The drill develops with runs
starting from different points so that the keeper can practice 1 v 1 from
different angles. A defender can be introduced to make the drill more
realistic but should start from behind the striker so that the keeper is
called into action.

The keeper looks to use the following techniques in a 1 v 1
situation:

- Use the bisector for positioning (note – if the striker is running from a very wide angle, the keeper may need to move outside the bisector to give extra protection to their near post.)
- The straighter the run, the further out the keeper heads;
- Unless the striker loses control, the keeper looks to make the save in the box. That way, they can use their hands;
- The keeper commits to making the save as late as possible;
- The keeper makes themselves as big as possible, making the goal seem small to the striker;
- Just prior to shooting the striker is likely to look down at the ball;
- The keeper aims to spread themselves as wide as possible, and so dives in a kind of forward star shape, arms and legs spread, body more upright than sideways. The Danish goalkeeper Peter Schmeichel was the master of the 1 v 1 situation. While usually the expectation is a goal in these situations, with Schmeichel, spectators expected to see a save. Find clips of him in 1 v 1 situations to see this 'star' dive in operation.

Eighty-Seven (Technique): Saving the ball away from trouble

There is little point making a spectacular diving save if the ball is then pushed straight into the path of an on-rushing striker, who nets into the empty goal. Keepers should aim to develop strong wrists and hands, so when making diving saves which they cannot hold, they push the ball away from goal and ideally out of play.

In this drill, shots are taken from three positions on the edge of the box. A stationary defender is used to create realism and some visual obstacle for the keeper. However, we do not want this defender to stop the shot reaching the target, as it is a goalkeeping practice. A mannequin if fine for the role of the defender. The other two strikers chase the ball in after the save.

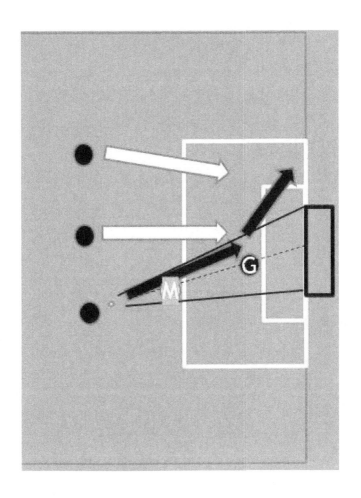

Dealing with Crosses

Eighty-Eight (Drill and Technique): Crosses

Practice receiving crosses and corners. Start unopposed. With youngsters, the ball can be lobbed in. As the skill level of the keeper develops, introduced kicked crosses and corners, plus strikers and defenders.

- The ball should be caught at the highest point it can be reached;
- If jumping, lead with the nearest leg to the direction of the cross;
- Leap with this leg bent and slightly forwards. The keeper is very vulnerable catching a cross as their arms and eyes are focussed on the ball. The raised knee offers some protection;
- Keep eyes on the ball. As the drill develops, and both attackers and defenders are involved, there will be a lot of movement around the keeper.
- Call clearly and early – 'Keeper's' or 'Smith's' - the keeper wants his team mates to recognise he is coming for the ball so that they can a) clear him a path to the ball; b) not jump in front of him and c) protect him from on-rushing strikers.
- The hands should be spread and behind the ball, with fingers pointing upwards;
- As the keeper lands, he or she brings the ball into their chest.

Eighty-Nine (Technique): Punching

It is not always possible to catch a cross. The ball may be too high to take comfortably; there may be too much jostling; conditions may be making the ball bobble and swerve.

In these situations, punching the ball is the sensible option. Strike the ball with the fist, rather than flapping with the hand. Aim for height and distance. Punch through the ball as though hitting a punchbag.

Corner and crossing drills are great opportunities for the keeper to practise their punching techniques.

Communication and Organisation

The keeper sees play better than any other player on the pitch. As such, they should take charge organising their defense, and instructing other players regarding danger, passing options and positional options.

The keeper might go long moments without touching the ball. That is especially true in the modern game where many teams like to play on the break, catching their opponents while they are out of their preferred defensive shape.

Shouting and communicating helps the keeper to maintain their concentration. It also helps them to keep warm, which is an important factor on cold winter mornings, especially with younger players.

Ninety (Technique): Communication

It is hard to find a specific drill from communication; however, it is something which should be practised whenever there is a drill with any objective which involves a keeper. When communicating, keepers should keep in mind:

- What to say;
- How to say it:
- When to say it.

What to say: The answer is something short. Clear, specific instructions are essential. 'Mark him,' is meaningless – the defense do not know who the 'him' is, and they are unclear who should be marking this unidentified threat. On the other hand – 'Dave, number 6' is very clear. Dave looks up, finds number 6, realises he is unmarked and resolves the problem quickly.

Similarly, instructions such as 'out', 'away', 'time' and so forth are clearly understood and not ambiguous.

How to say it: Clearly and firmly. Soccer pitches are noisy places, at least, they should be. Players are concentrating and will not be putting their efforts into trying to catch a mumbled instruction from their Number 1. However, we can add to that the idea of calmness. It is human nature to react badly to a screamed instruction. Young players in particular, with high voices and a lack of experience, can tend to screech instructions. The young keeper then wonders why his or her demand for the defense to push out was not met. The answer is that the said defense were fed up with being, as they see it, criticised by a manic keeper.

So loud? Yes; shouting is probably necessary just to be heard, but controlled volume works best.

When to say it: The primary purpose of giving instructions is to inform teammates and so help the team, the secondary purpose it to keep one's own concentration up. The best keepers manage to do both. They give clear, concise and useful instruction when it is needed. They switch this to encouragement when instruction is unnecessary or unhelpful. For example, trying to re-position a centre half when the centre forward is about to shoot is probably counter-productive; the advanced defender is watching the shot, the striker does not want to be distracted.

'Great pass' or 'Super shot' on the other hand is both encouraging to teammates without distracting them and helps to keep the goalie's own mind focussed.

The time to stop communicating is in a dead ball situation such as a penalty or attacking free kick, when the taker will be concentrating on hitting the ball correctly.

Having read this chapter, the key points to take are:

- Goalkeepers need to be physically and mentally strong (we will return to resilience in the next chapter)
- It is a technical role as well as an intuitive one, with positioning and technique key to success;
- Goalkeepers must communicate effectively;
- Their role in the modern game is sometimes as an extra outfield player as well as a shot stopper. Since this is an offensive role, we did not look at it in detail in this book, but the implication is that keepers should be involved in

the same outfield drills as outfield players, as well as their own specialised drills.

We have looked in a lot of detail about the physical, tactical and technical elements of defense and defenders. In the final chapter we will focus on the more nebulous but equally important attributes of all good defenses – mental fortitude.

The Qualities of Strong Defensive Players and a Strong Team Defense

We'll start this chapter with a short anecdote. We, the publishers of this book, received a forlorn sounding message the other day from a young coach who has just taken over the running of his U9 side.

Quite rightly, this coach believes it is important to coach his team to play soccer the right way. He wants to develop skills and technique, communication and teamwork. That, he has quickly realised, is often a matter not conducive to winning matches with young players. The problem, as we will realise, is that Under nines are just, under nine years of age. They make mistakes, errors of judgement and technique. It is how they learn to improve, whether in their schoolwork, in their social lives or on the soccer pitch.

This coach wants his team to play out from the back, to develop a passing game which will, as they become older, turn them into better and more effective soccer players. He is helping them to acquire the skills and understanding which will be in demand as they move up the soccer pyramid.

But his problem is that teams he faces have worked out that if they simply set up their team along the edge of the box, leaving a sweeper or two to clear up if the ball gets beyond this group. His team keeps conceding, morale is slipping and, no doubt, the ultra-competitive soccer moms and dads on the side-lines are becoming frustrated. In fact, since kids usually cope better with winning and losing than adults, it is probably their parents that are contributing to the falling confidence of the team.

There are no magic answers. Even at the highest levels of the game, coaches will seek short cuts to success or (more often) survival which delays the inevitable. Indeed, short termism is the plague of the modern game. Coaches being sacked after a short run of just moderate success; Maurizio Sarri, the Italian coach who spent a season with Chelsea, winning the Europa cup and achieving third place in the league (behind the huge spending Liverpool and Manchester City) was deemed to have failed to achieve enough, and was sacked.

But the U9 coach should take comfort from the fact that it is he that is correct. In the end, his team will come good and his players will thank him from teaching them properly.

Which leads us to the overwhelming, primary characteristic needed in every defensive player (and, for that matter, striker, midfielder, substitute, coach and, probably, fan.) Soccer players need resilience.

Knowing what resilience looks like is not too hard. Among other attributes of resilience are:

1) The ability to keep things in perspective;
2) The mental strength to face up to adversity;
3) The ability to work hard in preparation, seeing the bigger picture;
4) The ability to concentrate on the present, not get lost in the future or dwell in the past;
5) A positive outlook;
6) A focus on things we can control and influence, and an acceptance of those we cannot.

However, achieving this is tricky. Here are a couple of tips which work well. They also challenge the traditional concept of the coach as a hard giver of tough love; a man (or woman, but usually the former when it comes to soccer) who demands the earth and lets a player know if they are failing to deliver it.

Ninety-One (Technique) Developing resilience – The Law of Attraction

Coaches build up their teams. One of the challenges facing a new leader in any scenario is that their new team is in reality that which belongs to the old boss. This is true in business, in the professions, in retail as well as in sport.

Over time, the coach builds the team in their likeness. One of the conditions which might influence this selection is the law of attraction. Simply put, this law states that personality types are attracted to similar types. Thus, a player with a positive outlook and forward-looking philosophy will be naturally attracted to players with a similar outlook.

This is a very desirable cycle, since people of similarly positive outlooks create a rising spiral of goodwill and good feeling around them. Other people are drawn into their good attitude and develop that positivity themselves.

Feeling good about oneself is a crucial element of resilience. People with positive views of themselves – self-esteem as we would have called it in the old days – cope better with adversity. They recognise that failures occur and see them not as a personal reflection on their own character, but as an opportunity to learn and progress.

With a good sense of self-worth (but not arrogance, which is self-confidence without perspective) a player understands that criticism is not personal (and if it is, then it is not worth consideration) but a way of helping one to progress for the good of the team and the individual.

But there is a downside to the law of attraction. Because it applies as well when a player's outlook is negative. Negativity sucks the energy out of a team. It makes playing a chore rather than a pleasure – when that happens, training becomes an effort rather than something to which to look forward; confidence becomes fragile and team spirit thinly veneered. It takes just a small piece of adversity for it to fracture.

Therefore, the coach can use the law of attraction to build his squad; to ease out the most negative and promote the most positive, knowing that their influence will spread and grow, improving the resilience of the team. It is a long-term goal, but one which every coach should hold close to their heart.

Ninety-Two (Drill) Developing resilience through leadership

We are not sure that this is really a drill, although some exercises will help to develop leadership. The best teams are made up of leaders, not just a decision-making captain. The best leaders also know their limitations and understand when it is best to defer to another.

Thus, the wily old centre back might be the spiritual leader of the team, and wear the armband, but he will recognise that the young full back, barely out of short trousers, is better placed to make the call to push out for offside.

By recognising and supporting that young full back, even when he makes the occasional mistake, that player will grow in confidence himself, and contribute more to the team. He too will become a leader.

There are exercises and attitudes that can help to promote leadership:

- Visualisation exercise where lifting trophies, scoring penalties, making tackles are played through in the head, raising self-confidence;
- No blame environments where analysis of mistakes lays responsibility with the team rather than an individual – which is indeed usually the case.
- Training sessions where players are encouraged to experiment, and when something is attempted in a match, and fails to come off, the effort is rewarded rather than criticised;
- With younger players (this can be a little cringeworthy with adults and older girls and boys) de-briefs can end with circle of congratulation, where each player says something positive about every other player's contribution to the game.
- Creating an environment where every person's contribution is allowed, encouraged and valued - even if not always acted upon.

158

And, as a small bonus, here are three drills which all coache.. including our friend with the U9s, can use to develop playing out from the back.

Ninety-Three (Drill) Playing out from the back (1) Building Confidence

Here there is a five plus a keeper against two scenarios. Only the defense (in black as they are in possession) are allowed in the box. Outside the box are three grids. The two white opponents may move between the grids but only one is permitted in any grid at the same time. As many black players as required are needed.

The aim of the black team is to play the ball out of the grids to be an offensive move.

This drill will allow confidence to build as there is little pressure on the ball and will also teach the value of getting the ball wide and switching play. It will show young players that, in this situation, passing is better than dribbling.

As the players improve their skills and technique, extra opponents can be introduced.

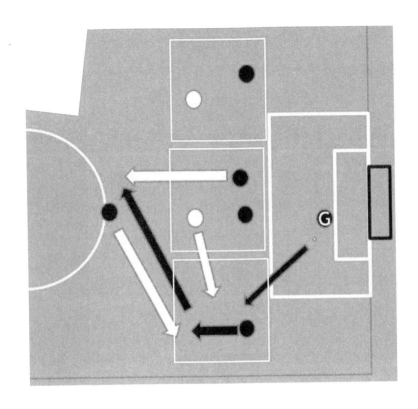

Ninety- Four (Drill) Playing out from the back (2)

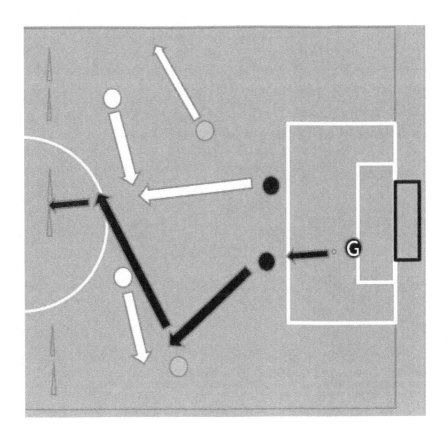

This more complex drill includes a defensive aspect if play breaks down. Again, it encourages movement, passing and getting the ball wide.

The black team aim to pass the ball any of the three narrow 'goals'; the whites aim to score. The grey pair act as full backs for the defense, but if transition occurs, they become wide players for the offence.

Encourage players to make use of the space. A good first touch makes this easier. Firm passing along the ground makes that first touch easier to achieve.

Ninety-Five (Tactic) Playing out from the back (3)

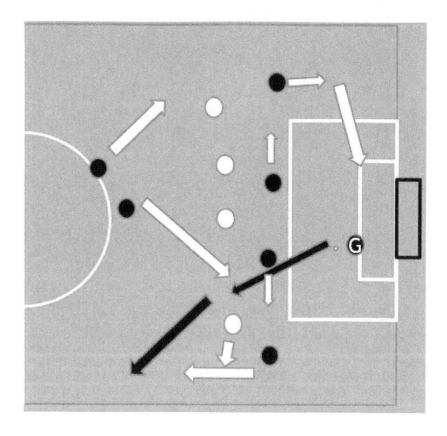

This kind of movement will create space. At the point of kicking, the two central defenders split. One full back pushes on, the other retreats into the box for the short pass. (If this does not work, try sending both full backs into the box for the short pass. Under the new

162

rules relating to goal kicks, they will have time before opponents can close them down.)

One of the strikers drops into the hole created by the central defenders to be available to receive the goal kick. If the white markers are doing their job, they will have moved with the centre backs, if not the centre backs will have time to receive the pass.

The ball needs to be shifted quickly, so the second pass is down the line to a player running there – either the full back advancing, or the other striker moving laterally.

Lots of practice will get even a young team playing this efficiently. Soon, variations can be built in, such as one of the centre backs dropping into the box, and both full backs pushing wide for the pass. However, with young players, there will be errors in the early days as they develop their confidence on the ball. If we, as coaches, accept this but continue to encourage, our players will progress more in the long run than those in teams whose only philosophies are kick it long and crowd out the opponents.

They will still be trying to play like this when they are U11s, while the players taught properly will be running rings around them.

Ninety-Six (Tactics) Identifying potential defenders

We can keep this short, because everybody is a potential player in defense. No longer is it necessary to be 6' 4" to play at centre half since the game is more about speed and control than hitting it long and hoping.

We think that the issue of the past – that playing in defense was somehow unglamorous – is no longer the case. But where it is, it can be sold in that everybody in the team has a defensive role, but they also have an offensive one.

Having said that, there is no doubt that some young players just love defending. They like the fact that they are facing the opposition; they enjoy the physical side, and they like the fact that often they have a little more time on the ball. There is definitely a satisfaction in keeping a clean sheet.

Our top tactics for spotting defenders are easy:

1) See who enjoys playing there!
2) In practice matches and drills, operate a policy of switching positions. There is nothing but good to be gained from a striker learning the issues of playing centre half – and vice versa. Indeed, players improve from learning about the challenges facing their direct opponents. Who knows, that

wide midfielder who just doesn't quite make it as a regular starter in that position, might turn out to be a wonder at full back.

Ninety-Seven (Drills): Trial for defense (1)

When we are holding direct trials for new players, we should focus on looking for players with the key attributes of that position:

1) Run speed tests – a good defender needs pace;
2) Check basic techniques such as first touch, passing and heading the ball, where heading forms a part of the game;
3) Place the trialist in challenging situations, such as several spells acting as an outnumbered defender in rondo drills; see how they react to this. A defender needs resilience; if they get fed up, feeling they are not getting the chance to show what they can do, then they probably lack the resilience to be a top defender.

Ninety-Eight (Drill): Trial for defense (2)

However, since reading the game is a vital skill for a defender, and this is hard to test in a 'drill' situation; then a match situation is the place to check for this.

A match trial also gives the opportunity for a coach to see which defensive players have a natural affinity for each other, complementing their teammates' strengths and compensating for their weakness.

The best defense is not necessarily made up of the best four or five individual defenders.

Ninety-Nine (Tactic): Ensuring consistency in defense

Finally, more than any other aspect of soccer, defense is improved through repetition. The back line needs to know how each player works. Nevertheless, injuries occur, and players become unavailable for a multitude of reasons.

Back up players need to be able to fit into the defensive system being played. For example, in a side where a central defender comes out a lot, and a full back fills in, to put in a replacement who likes to bomb forward will not be a good idea, however strong an individual that player is.

The way for the coach to get the best out of his defensive squad is to get them to play together regularly, try to keep a settled side, but ensure that back up players also get their chance to learn the team formations and defensive tactics. It seems obvious, but in a tight training programme, where a coach is looking to maximise the effectiveness of his first choice defense, it is easy to overlook that this may not always be available. Reserves need to slot in smoothly...and readily.

The points we wish to emphasise in this chapter are:

- Mental strength and resilience are as important in a defender as specific skills;
- The same is true for the whole defense, who must work together effectively, and, in a way, which complements each other;
- It is good to play out from the back, especially in a modern game where the target man type striker is a dying breed;
- Back up players must be able to fit in easily when needed, and this involves ensuring training supports this need;
- When holding trials to find the best defense, look for the skills of a soccer player first and foremost, resilience should follow as an equal partner and the ability to fit into the team structure is also essential.

Conclusion

The role of the player for whom defense is their main responsibility has become more glamorous. Defenders and goalkeepers are now being transferred in the professional game for $100 million and more.

Youngsters wear the name of Van Dijk, Maguire, Umtiti, Koulibaly, Pique and Godin on the back of their replica shirts. The names of Neymar Jr, Pepe, Griezmann and Messi might still sell more shirts, but the gap is narrowing.

In the old days, boys and girls wanted to be strikers – the glory position. But now the role of the defense is much higher profile, and just as important in the success of a team. There is no struggle with our under eights to find players willing to play at the back. That is a good thing. No longer is it the domain of the over large child who could kick it miles... but who lacked skill, pace and creativity.

Nevertheless, learning to be a defender, and improving in that position, is down to training and repetition more than genius and unpredictability. A mercurial defender is an oxymoron. Therefore, drills for defense do need greater input from a coach than those for strikers or for midfield play. The need for players to work on defense in training is paramount in a successful team. The motivation they can find for doing so less easy to come by. Playing defense is thrilling, training for the position can, in the wrong hands, be much less so. Which leads us neatly onto our final point:

One Hundred (Tactic): The best coaches make defense training fun.

There's no more to say about this one.

The end… almost!

Reviews are not easy to come by.

As an independent author with a tiny marketing budget, I rely on readers, like you, to leave a short review on Amazon.

Even if it's just a sentence or two!

So if you enjoyed the book, please head to the product page, and leave a review as shown below.

I am very appreciative for your review as it truly makes a difference.

Thank you from the bottom of my heart for purchasing this book and reading it to the end.

Printed in Great Britain
by Amazon